# The Workbook of Darkroom Techniques
John Hedgecoe

**Focal Press**
Boston • Oxford • Johannesburg • Melbourne • New Delhi

# CONTENTS

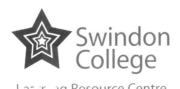

**The Workbook of Darkroom Techniques**

*21st March, 2007*
*5405000270850*

Focal Press is an imprint of Butterworth–Heinemann.

© 1985, 1997 Octopus Publishing Group Ltd.
Text © 1985, 1997 Octopus Publishing Group Ltd. and John Hedgecoe
Photographs © 1978, 1979, 1980, 1983, 1984 and 1997 John Hedgecoe
Reprinted 1988
First paperback edition 1990, reprinted 1994
Revised and updated 1997

Typeset by Dorchester Typesetting Group Ltd, Dorchester, Dorset, England

| | |
|---|---|
| Editor | Frank Wallis |
| Associate author | John Farndon |
| Consultant art editor | Mel Peterson |
| Art editor | Zoe Davenport |
| Production | Jean Rigby |
| Artists | Stan North, Sandra Pond, Kai Choi, Kuo Kang Chen |

| | |
|---|---|
| Revised edition | |
| Contributing editor | Chris George |
| Senior editor | Penelope Cream |
| Editor | Cathy Lowne |
| Production controller | Rachel Lynch |
| Digital manipulation | Glen Wilkins |

| | |
|---|---|
| Executive editor | Judith More |
| Executive art editor | Janis Utton |

ISBN 0-240-80321-3

The publisher offers special discounts on bulk orders of this book.
For information, please contact:
Manager of Special Sales
Butterworth–Heinemann
225 Wildwood Avenue
Woburn, MA 01801-2041
Tel: 617-928-2500
Fax: 617-928-2620

For information on all Focal Press publications available, contact our World Wide Web home page at:
http://www.focalpress.com

10 9 8 7 6 5 4 3 2 1
Printed in China

# Introduction

Photographic creativity does not end in the split second that the shutter is open. True, there is not much that can be done to make an arresting image from a picture that was taken with a maximum of error and a minimum of flair: the more competent you are in handling your camera, the more you develop an eye for form, tone, composition, colour, mood, atmosphere and the idea behind the picture, the more successful you will be. But a great

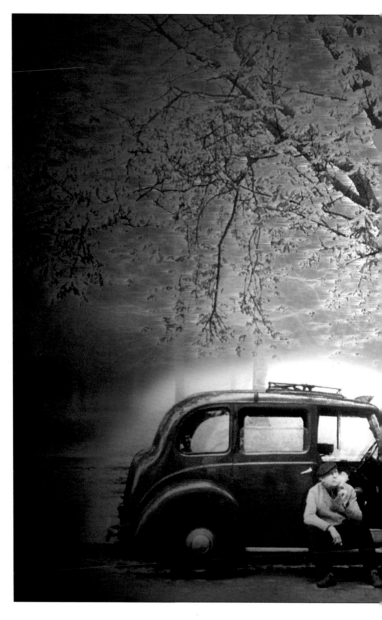

deal of the pleasure in photography, as well as a long stretch of the path to success, begins once the film is removed from the camera. The darkroom is an alchemist's laboratory, where the base metal of the prosaic can be turned into the gold of the unusual, mistakes can be rectified, reality manipulated and your personal vision given expression. The following pages introduce some of the techniques with which you can achieve those ends.

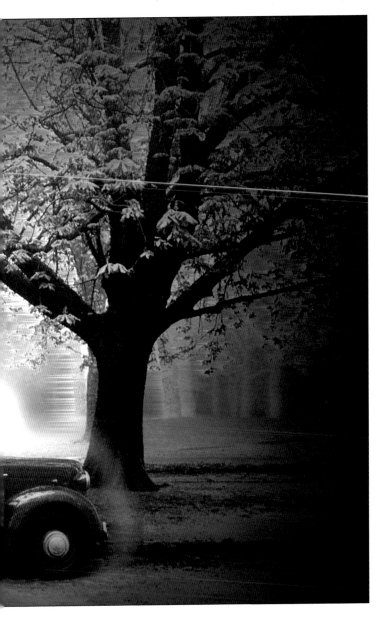

# The Dry Area

You do not need a proper darkroom for any of the techniques described in this book. All can be attempted successfully in an improvised darkroom in a bathroom, bedroom or garage. But even if your workspace is makeshift, your organization must not be. Disorder does not stop you getting results, but it can stop you getting first-class results. Plan the layout of your darkroom carefully, separating each operation as much as possible. The most important division is between the 'wet' bench where chemicals are used and the 'dry' bench for all procedures that do not need chemicals, such as enlarging.

The illustration below shows one way of organizing a dry area. It is designed to face the wet bench layout overleaf. Very few items of equipment are essential, except for the enlarger, but you will find scissors, tape, scalpel and rulers far more useful than you imagined. The pinboard keeps them to hand, and easy to put away. Notice how the safelight is mounted over the cutting board, where you need to see well.

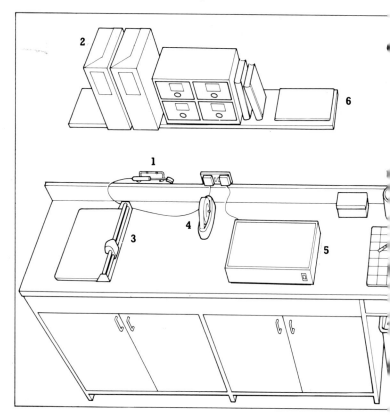

1. Tacking iron
2. Files and records
3. Print trimmer
4. Masking tape dispenser
5. Light box

6. Negative file
7. Safelight
8. Pinboard
9. Retouching brushes
10. Rulers, scissors, tape, notepad

● **If space is restricted** and you cannot separate wet and dry benches, divide the printing and processing areas with a partition or splash board to protect the enlarger and paper.

● **Raise the enlarger** on a plinth if space is so restricted that you cannot erect a partition to separate it from the wet bench. This helps to keep splashes off the enlarger baseboard. Be sure that the enlarger is supported firmly.

● **Electrical equipment** should be in the dry area unless it is designed for the wet area and has the necessary safety features.

● **Mount the sockets** for the enlarger, meters, etc., just above bench height.

● **Paint the wall** behind the enlarger matt black to cut down the effects of light from the negative carrier. Paint the other walls white for maximum light.

● **Mount shelves** above both wet and dry benches to keep small items of equipment to hand. Round off corners and do not mount shelves near the enlarger – it is easy to bump your head.

● **You can buy luminous spots** for shelves or workbench edges to help you to find your way around the darkroom.

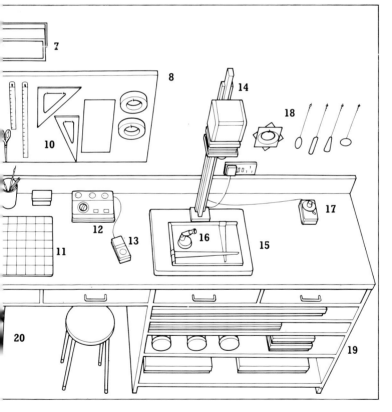

11. Scalpel and cutting board
12. Colour analyser
13. Meter probe
14. Enlarger with colour head
15. Easel with adjustable masks

16. Focusing magnifier
17. Exposure timer
18. Printing masks
19. Storage space for print paper
20. Waste bin

# The Wet Area

All processing and chemical mixing should take place in a separate wet area. You can get processing sinks, made of polypropylene, PVC or glass-fibre. These contain spillages and are easy to wash down after processing, but if you are careful you can get away with processing on a flat bench, providing the sink is reasonably nearby and the area is well cordoned off. Cover the surface of the bench in plastic laminate to protect it from chemicals, and erect a splashback to protect the wall and a rim at the front.

The illustration below shows one possible way of organizing the wet bench. It is designed to face the dry bench on pages 8–9. The processing sequence would normally run from left to right along the bench. Prints come from the enlarger on the left (page 9), into the developing tray, into the wash tray and fixing trays, arranged in a row along the bench, and then into the sink. This arrangement suits most right-handed people. Left-handed people may prefer to organize the bench in the opposite direction.

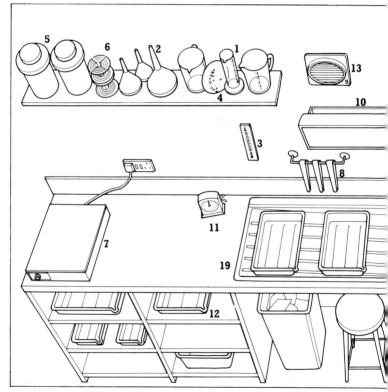

1. Graduates and measuring jugs
2. Funnels
3. Thermometer
4. Sponge
5. Film-processing tanks
6. Spirals
7. Tray warmer
8. Print tongs
9. Print processing drum
10. Safelight with string pull

● **If space is very restricted**, arrange the three black-and-white print processing trays in a tier on shelves.

● **A water supply and sink** are not essential since you can keep fresh water in tanks and take films and prints out to a sink. But water on tap and a place to drain solutions make life infinitely easier.

● **A bright safelight** is essential. You need to see clearly for black-and-white printing in particular.

● **Arrange the switch** for the main room light on a string pull that is easily accessible from both wet and dry areas.

The string means you can switch the light on even with wet hands.

● **Ventilate the area** around the wet bench properly.

● **Store chemicals** well away from the dry area of the darkroom.

● **With a light-tight print drum** or deep tank slot processor you can even process prints without a proper wet area; an ordinary sink will do. But if you process prints or films in the kitchen sink, be sure that spillages cannot contaminate food or eating utensils.

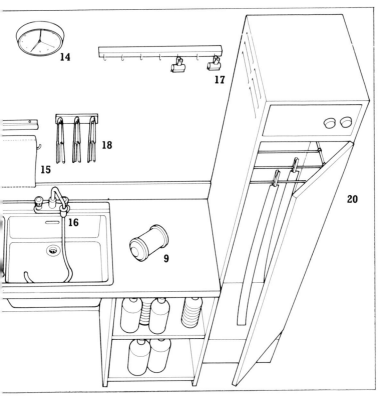

11. Process timer
12. Storage space for trays
13. Ventilation fan
14. Clock that can be read by safelight
15. Paper towels

16. Water filter
17. Clips
18. Squeegees
19. Draining board
20. Film-drying cabinet

# Routes to the Print

The plan below shows the major steps on the route to the final print using each of the three main types of film: black-and-white film, colour negative or print film, and colour slide or reversal film. In each case, the first step is the same – loading the exposed film into a light-proof processing tank.

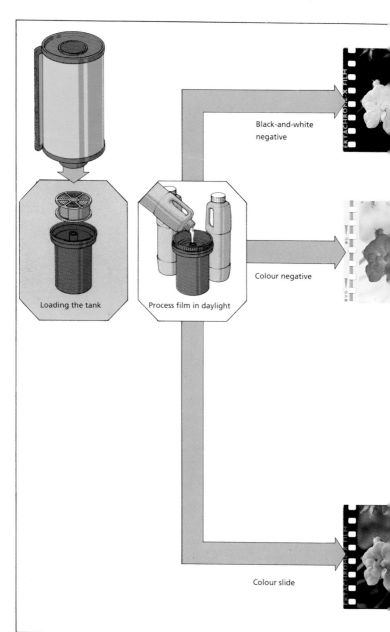

Black-and-white negative

Colour negative

Loading the tank

Process film in daylight

Colour slide

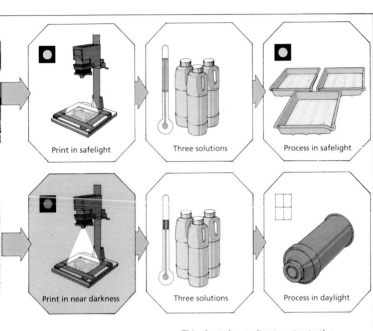

Print in safelight — Three solutions — Process in safelight

Print in near darkness — Three solutions — Process in daylight

This chart shows direct routes to the print, but there are many other possibilities. For example, by copying a slide onto negative film, you can make a print using negative paper, which is cheaper than the reversal paper used for making prints from slides. It is possible to make monochrome prints directly from colour negatives, and, by copying, from slides.

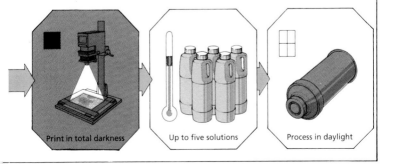

Print in total darkness — Up to five solutions — Process in daylight

# Changing the Image

A photographer often feels the need to manipulate an image in some way, even if only to crop to improve composition. Manipulation can be as simple as local exposure control (known as dodging and burning) or as complicated as colour separations: you can only change an image partly or create an entirely new one.

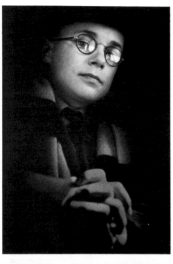

### Local exposure control
By using masks to cover certain areas of the print during exposure, you can exert very precise control over the final appearance of the picture. Techniques include: burning in (page 58–9); dodging (page 60); contrast control (page 61); vignetting (pages 62–3) and perspective control (pages 64–5).

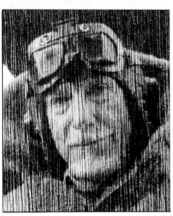

### Texture effects
You can give prints a different 'texture' in a variety of ways: by printing on different types of paper (glossy, smooth, matt, eggshell and so on); by covering the print with texture screens during exposure (pages 88–9); and even by making prints on a variety of surfaces (pages 112–13).

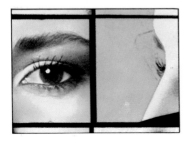

### Print finishing
The finished print can be manipulated in a variety of ways. Prints can be retouched to disguise blemishes or to repair defects (pages104–5); coloured by hand with dyes and paints (pages 106–7); spray-painted with an airbrush (pages 108–9); and dipped in toning baths to change their colour completely (pages 110–111).

## Separation techniques

Many effects and techniques depend on separating an image into its various components and then recombining these in different ways. Colour images can be split into their colour components (colour separation pages 118–19); black-and-white images into tonal components (tone separation page 120). Techniques include posterization (pages 120–121).

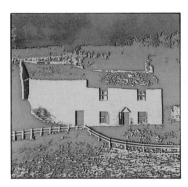

## Special materials

By copying the original image onto alternative photographic materials you can create a wide range of effects. Lith film, which reduces an image to pure black and pure white, and eliminates all tones of grey, is particularly useful (pages 88–9). It can be used in all the separation techniques, and for effects such as 'neons' (pages 128–9). Other interesting special materials include equidensity film (pages 122–3).

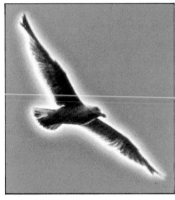

## Combining images

Different photographs can be combined on the same print in an enormous number of ways. Combination techniques include: exposing the various negatives onto the same print (pages 94–5); montaging different prints (pages 96–101); creating mandalas (pages 126–7) and making different transfers onto the same print (page 83). Computer programs are now readily available that allow you create many of the same effects (pages 130–131).

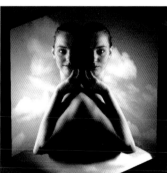

## Process variations

Some of the most startling effects are created by deliberately breaking the well-established rules of the process routine. Seeming accidents can be turned into creative tools. Prints can be processed in the wrong chemicals or fogged during development to produce striking 'solarized' images (pages 90–3).

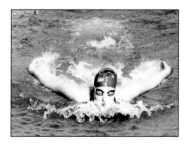

# Darkroom Chemistry

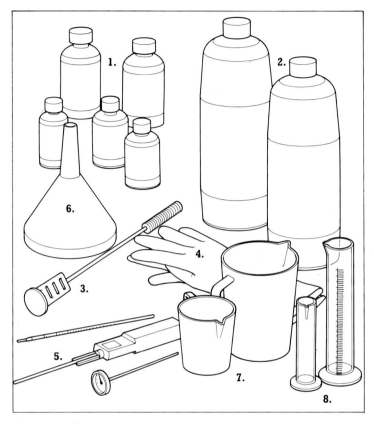

**What you need**

1. Glass storage bottles
2. Plastic storage bottles
3. Stirring rod
4. Rubber gloves
5. Thermometers
6. Funnel
7. Mixing jugs
8. Graduates

● **Buy a range of graduates** and mixing jugs, such as 1000ml, 250ml and 50ml sizes. The 1000ml is fine for measuring bulk liquids but is not sufficiently accurate for concentrated liquid developers.

● **Use different jugs** for each chemical, if you can, to prevent contamination. Otherwise, you must clean the jug thoroughly before you mix the next solution. Always use a different jug for bleach.

● **Never use kitchen measures** for chemicals. Not only are they insufficiently accurate for photographic work, but they might also be corroded by certain chemicals and, more importantly, they might accidentally be used for measuring food afterwards.

● **Use a plastic funnel** for pouring chemicals into bottles. Make sure that the funnel has an air vent to prevent blow-back from rapid filling.

● **Wear rubber gloves** when mixing toxic and corrosive chemicals such as those found in bleaches, intensifying and reducing baths and some Ilfochrome chemicals. Surgeons' gloves, which are made of thinner material and give you more grip, are better still.

● **Measure temperatures** with the right thermometer. Spirit thermometers are inexpensive and accurate enough for black-and-white work. For high-temperature colour you need a mercury or electronic thermometer.

● **Protect** a mercury thermometer by using it as a reference only. Use a spirit thermometer for your routine work, but calibrate it against the mercury thermometer. Stand both thermometers side by side in a water bath. Check the temperature on each and write the results down – they will probably be slightly different. Now add warm water, raising the temperature of the bath half a degree at a time. Write down the reading on each thermometer at every step and plot the results on a simple graph. Use the graph to find the true reading of the spirit thermometer.

● **Store chemicals** as recommended by the maker or in proper storage jars.

● **Keep storage jars full.** The more air there is in the jar, the shorter the life of the solutions will be. Use an adjustable concertina jar to suit the volume of solution, reduce the air space by adding marbles, or top up the jar with an inert gas from a spray (eg Tetenal Protectan), which prevents oxidation.

### How long chemicals keep

|  | Working solution | Stock sol. in half-full bottles | Stock sol. in full bottles |
|---|---|---|---|
| **Black-and-white developers** | | | |
| Universal developer | 1 month | 3 months | 6 months |
| Fine-grain film developer | 1 month | 2 months | 6 months |
| High contrast film developer (stock) | 1 month | 2 months | 6 months |
| Standard paper developer* | 1 day | 2 months | 6 months |
| New generation black-and-white developer* | 1 day | 3 months | 1 year |
| **Black-and-white fixers and stops** | | | |
| Fixer* | 1 day | 1 month | 2 months |
| Stop bath* | 1 day | no limit | no limit |
| **Colour film chemicals** | | | |
| Negative developer | 4 weeks | 4 weeks | 4 weeks |
| bleach | no limit | no limit | no limit |
| fixer | 8 weeks | 8 weeks | 8 weeks |
| Colour slide film first developer | 4 weeks | 1 week | 8 weeks |
| colour developer | 8 weeks | 6 weeks | 12 weeks |
| bleach-fix | 24 weeks | 24 weeks | 24 weeks |
| **Colour print chemicals** | | | |
| Negative/positive developer | –** | 2 weeks | 4 weeks |
| stop bath | –** | 8 weeks | 8 weeks |
| bleach-fix | –** | 4 weeks | 4 weeks |
| Positive/positive first developer | – | 1 week | 2 weeks |
| colour developer | – | 1 week | 4 weeks |
| bleach-fix | – | 2 weeks | 6 weeks |
| Ilfochrome developer | – | – | 4 weeks |
| bleach | – | – | 4 months |
| fixer | – | – | 6 months |

* Keeping times for black-and-white paper chemicals at working strength are shown for solutions left in open processing trays.
** Colour print chemicals will keep for up to 2 weeks in deep tanks with floating lids.

# Mixing Chemicals

You can still make up a few useful solutions from 'raw' chemicals, but there is little point. Commercial formulas do the job more conveniently, more efficiently, and often more cheaply, too. And for many processes, only the commercial formula will give acceptable results. So, for all but a few special applications, photographic chemicals are made up from convenient, easy-to-mix commercial packages. These come in the form of either liquid concentrates or in packets of powder. Liquid chemicals are very easy to use. The working solution is made simply by diluting some of the concentrate in water. Powdered chemicals can be cheaper, but are slightly less easy to use and the whole packet must usually be used at once. Procedures for mixing both types are outlined below.

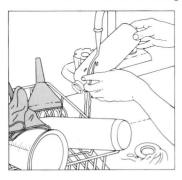

**1** Wash all the containers and mixing equipment thoroughly under running water. Use ordinary household detergent to help clean stubborn stains, never anything stronger. Arrange the chemicals in the order in which they are to be used.

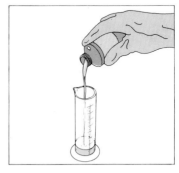

**2** When mixing very concentrated liquid chemicals, such as wetting agent, start by diluting the concentrate in a small graduate. You can then add this less concentrated solution to the full quantity of water in a larger jar to give the right dilution.

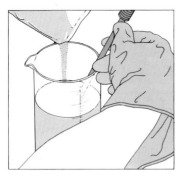

**5** With powdered chemicals, add the entire contents of each packet to the water in the specified order. Stir the solution gently all the time to help dissolve the powder. Wait until each chemical is completely dissolved before adding the next packet of powder.

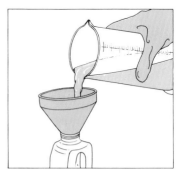

**6** If you are not using the solution immediately, store it in a proper storage bottle. Place a funnel in the neck and slowly pour in the mixed solution. Fill to the top to exclude air and thus extend the solution's life, or replace any air with an inert gas. Close the lid tightly.

● **Always add chemicals to water**, NEVER the other way round. This is especially important with chemicals containing acids.

● **Water filters,** whether activated carbon or magnetic, should be used for consistency when processing film.

● **Use all the packet** with powdered chemicals. Never try to make smaller quantities of solution by using a fraction of the packet. Some chemicals are added to the pack in a certain order so that they completely mix only when the solution is made up.

● **Clean equipment thoroughly**

● **Never use strong cleaners** such as bleach; they may contaminate the container.

● **Remove ingrained stains** with special darkroom cleaners.

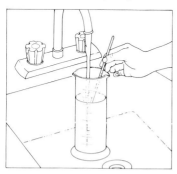

**3** Measure the water into a large graduate – this must be at least 20ml bigger than the total volume of the made-up solution. Check the temperature of the water and adjust if necessary. This is especially important with powdered chemicals.

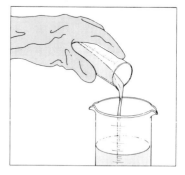

**4** If you are using liquid concentrates for colour chemicals and bleaches, you should remember to wear rubber gloves. Pour the entire contents of the bottle, or a measured amount as directed by the manufacturers, into the water and stir.

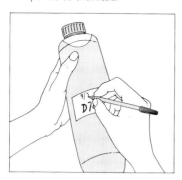

**7** Label the bottle clearly, using a waterproof marker. Either write directly on the bottle or use an adhesive label. Mark the exact name of the solution, the dilution and the date of preparation. Wipe the bottle clean and store at room temperature in the dark.

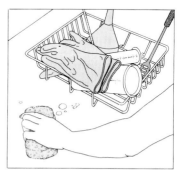

**8** Wash all the mixing equipment thoroughly in water or a proprietary darkroom cleanser. Remember to clean gloves, stirrer and thermometer as well as mixing jugs. Wipe down all the mixing surfaces immediately with a detergent-soaked sponge.

# Film Processors

If you want to process film, you must have a light-proof processing tank. For 35mm and roll film, you need a spiral tank. This is a cylindrical type, made either of stainless steel or plastic, containing a reel with a spiral groove to hold the film in place. For sheet film, however, you need three deep tank processors, or a film insert for a print drum.

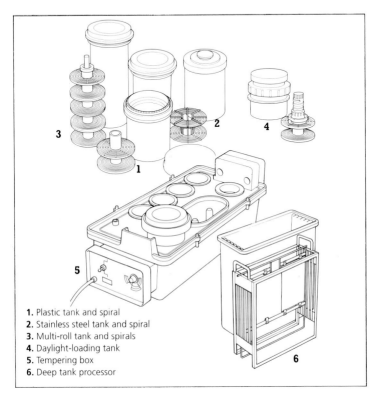

1. Plastic tank and spiral
2. Stainless steel tank and spiral
3. Multi-roll tank and spirals
4. Daylight-loading tank
5. Tempering box
6. Deep tank processor

● **Plastic or stainless steel?**
Plastic tanks are often a better bet for the beginner. They are cheap and robust, and the spiral is self-loading. But for the more experienced, a stainless steel tank may be more useful. The spiral is harder to load, but the film is less prone to sticking, and the tank may be dried in an oven for rapid reuse.

● **Multi-roll tanks** can save time and money if you often have many films to process at once.

● **Daylight-loading tanks** have special spirals that allow film to be loaded in normal light. This is perfect for the photographer who processes only the occasional roll, but their thirst for chemicals makes them uneconomical for regular use.

● **For regular colour work,** where accurate temperature control is paramount, it may be worth buying a thermostatically controlled 'tempering box' to keep both tank and chemicals at the right temperature.

● **Deep tank processors** can be made of either plastic or rubber. You must have a plastic tank for processing colour sheet film: colour-process chemicals attack rubber.

# Print Processors

All you need to process black-and-white prints is three open trays. You can process colour prints in open trays, but this means working in almost total darkness. For colour printing you need a light-proof processing tank into which all the chemicals can be poured in turn. Tanks range from hand-rolled drums to motorized, temperature-controlled processors.

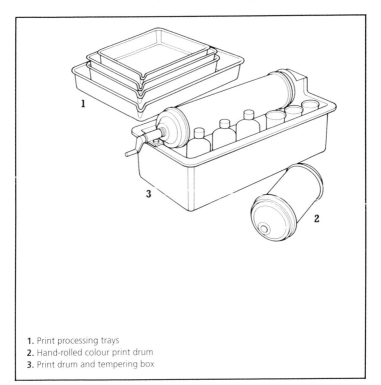

1. Print processing trays
2. Hand-rolled colour print drum
3. Print drum and tempering box

● **Buy three trays** for black-and-white print processing, a different colour for each of the three solutions (developer, wash and fixer), and always use same tray for each solution.

● **The simplest colour print drums** are agitated by merely rolling them along the bench. This is fine if you have the time and patience to ensure consistent agitation.

● **Deep tank processors** must be used in the dark, or under a colour-safe safelight, but this method is fives times quicker than drum processing.

● **A motorized drum** is a worthwhile investment if you do a great deal of colour printing, since it saves time and ensures that print agitation is repeatable and precise.

● **Tempering boxes** take the sweat out of maintaining the accurate temperature control vital in colour print processing. If you are using a room-temperature colour printing set, you should need a tempering box only in the coldest winters.

# The Enlarger

Darkroom work revolves around the enlarger, and making the right choice· is crucial. Buy the best that you can afford. But bear in mind that, given an equivalent lens, you can make prints on the most basic enlarger to match any made on a top-of-the-range model. For variable contrast printing, you will find that using a special variable control (VC) head is much quicker and more accurate than using individual filters. An expensive enlarger is not a guarantee of high-quality results. Rather, it offers a range of facilities that allow you to concentrate on making perfect prints.

● **Vertical enlargers**, in which the light is directly above the lens, make a good first buy. Their simple construction makes them noticeably cheaper than the reflex type.

● **Reflex enlargers**, in which the light is mounted horizontally and reflected through the lens from a mirror, are generally more compact and less prone to overheating than the traditional vertical type.

● **For black-and-white prints**, the best enlarger light source is a condenser. Condenser enlargers use lenses above the negative to concentrate the light, boosting contrast and cutting exposure times.

● **For colour prints**, you really need a diffuser enlarger unless you are prepared to go to great lengths to keep down dust. Hard condenser light highlights dust and scratches on the film. Diffuser enlargers have a ground glass screen to scatter and soften the light, disguising blemishes. With black and white, the gain in contrast with a condenser makes up for the effort needed to deal with dust. With colour, there is no gain in contrast, and a diffuser is a much better bet.

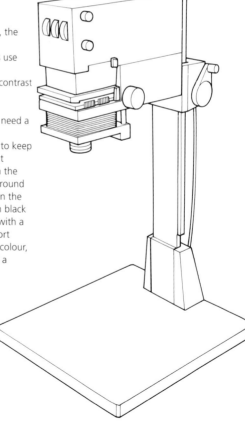

For colour printing, the colour of the enlarger light must be individually tailored for each picture to give correct colour. This is achieved by slotting coloured filters into the light path (subtractive printing) or, in very rare cases, by using red, green and blue combination lamps (additive printing). Most enlargers have some facility for colour correction ranging from a simple filter drawer to 'dial-in' heads for colour or VC black-and-white printing.

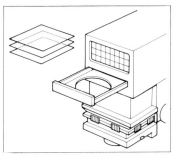

▲ The most basic system for colour correction is a drawer above the negative carrier that accepts inexpensive square acetate filters. Correction is usually subtractive and yellow, magenta and cyan filters of varying density are made up into individual 'filter packs' for each picture. The system is cheap and simple, and works just as well as more expensive methods. But operation is slow and tedious.

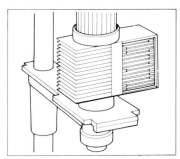

▲ One step up from the filter drawer is a filter panel, although these are not often of high quality. The filter panel is a large box set between the lamp and the negative carrier. It contains 14 filters (including a UV filter) which can be slid into the light path to give the right colour balance. The system is effective and much less effort to use than the filter drawer, but the restricted range of filters in the panel limits its scope.

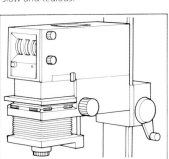

▲ Enlargers with dial-in colour heads are best for colour printing, although these are more expensive. Dial-in heads usually have 'dichroic' filters in yellow, magenta and cyan that can be dialled progressively into the light path to fine tune the colour balance. Dichroic filters work by interference, not absorption, and are very resistant to fading, but it is worth doing colour checks to see if the lamp bulb is fading with age.

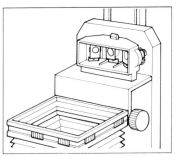

▲ Enlargers based on the additive principle have three light sources (blue, green and red), and colour correction is achieved by varying the brightness of each light. They are generally expensive, and the system is harder to grasp than the subtractive. But they give finer control over colour balance, and it is much easier to create special effects such as solarization and printing black-and-white negatives in colour.

# Enlarger Movements

Once you have decided on your price range and the type of enlarger you need, look at models and facilities. An important feature is solid construction: a shortcoming of cheaper enlargers is vibration during exposure. A solid, well-engineered column and head are the first steps on the road to quality prints. You should also ensure that the column is mounted on a solid surface.

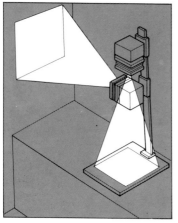

● **Look for interchangeable heads**. They make it easier to upgrade from black and white to VC and colour, and also mean you can use the right head for the job without having two complete enlargers. A condenser head ideal for black-and-white work can be replaced in minutes with a colour head.

● **A tilting head** can be very useful if you often make large prints. This can often make up for a short enlarger column. By tilting the head at an angle of 90° to the column (pictured left), you can project a much bigger image on the wall than is possible on the baseboard.

● **Inclined columns** allow very large images to be projected clear of the base of the column.

● **A tall column** is far more convenient to use than a tilting head for making many large prints, but making a tall column rigid is expensive. In addition, the masking frame may butt against the column in big blow-ups.

● **Double tube columns** give a much firmer support for the enlarger head. Rectangular box columns offer even firmer support.

● **Friction brakes** are a cheap, simple way of locking the enlarger head on the column, but the head is harder to position accurately and not totally secure.

● **Rack and pinion systems** allow you to crank the head up and down the column precisely and securely and in a smooth movement – but they cost more.

● **A wall-mounted enlarger** (left) is very rigid and allows you to vary the print size accurately over a much wider range than a bench-top enlarger.

# Enlarger Lenses

Enlarger lenses are built differently from camera lenses, so they give good resolution and contrast at even small apertures. The enlarger lens is the ultimate control on the quality of your prints, so get the best you can afford. No amount of technique can make up for an inferior lens.

● **If your enlarger has a lens** fitted when you buy it, do not assume that this is the best for you. Enlarger manufacturers have to compromise to meet all kinds of demands.

● **Three-element lenses** are relatively inexpensive, but they rarely give very high resolution and are prone to vignetting – that is, darkening of the image away from the centre.

● **Look for edge definition.** It is at the edge of the image, not the centre, that poorer quality lenses fall down.

● **Watch out for vignetting** if you plan to print from slides. The high contrast of slides shows up vignetting all too distinctly. It can be reduced by stopping down, but this can mean overlong exposures.

● **Choose the focal length** to fit the format of the films that you use and the size of enlargements that you plan to make. Focal length is a compromise between quality and convenience. Long focal lengths give best results; short focal lengths are easier to use because they give a bigger image at a given enlarger head height. The lens must be wide enough to cover the film format without loss of quality. Look for a focal length similar to the diagonal of the film format. A 50mm lens is fine for 35mm negatives; 6 x 6cm (2¼in) negatives need an 80mm lens.

● **Do not get a lens** that is too short for the format. Wide-angle lenses may perform well only at magnifications more suitable for a larger format.

● **Some wide-angle enlarger lenses** have been constructed to perform well even with small format films. They are, however, expensive.

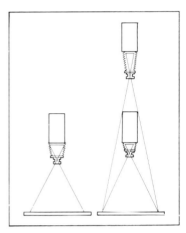

▲ Matching the focal length to the film diagonal gives the best possible results, but can mean that the enlarger head has to be raised high for large prints from small-format film (above right).

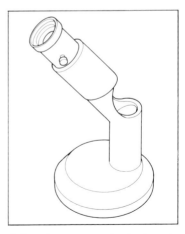

▲ Even the most expensive six-element lens will not give good results if focused badly, so it is worth buying a focus magnifier to help to achieve maximum sharpness. The magnification means that you focus on the film grain.

# Timers and Meters

Precision control is vital in many aspects of darkroom work, and there are many aids on the market to help you achieve the accuracy needed: timers to time processes and exposures; exposure meters to determine the exposure for each print; and colour analysers to help find the filtration for perfect colour balance in a colour print. Only a basic timer is essential, but each item of equipment takes a little of the tedium out of darkroom work and helps maintain the consistency essential for quality results.

● **Basic universal timers**, giving times in both minutes and seconds, are enough for routine black-and-white work. But their limitations become clear in colour processing sequences.

● **Colour processing** often involves many steps, each of different length, and a special process timer can be invaluable. Even the most basic process timer has the facility to time each stage in a long and varied sequence.

● **A bleep timer** is the cheapest form of exposure timer. It emits an audible bleep every second, leaving you free to concentrate on burning in and dodging.

● **Programmable timers** are expensive but switch the enlarger on and off for you, thus ensuring completely accurate exposure timing, leaving you free to concentrate on local exposure variations.

● **An enlarger timer** that can be operated by a foot-switch will make dodging and burning in much easier.

● **Dual-purpose timers** combine the functions of process and exposure timers in one unit, but can cost a great deal of money.

● **Exposure meters** save time and money on test strips by indicating how much exposure each print will need. Meters that give an 'integrated' reading from the whole picture area are quicker to use and cheaper, but are also less precise. With the more expensive 'spot' meters, you can take readings from chosen areas of the picture for precision exposures.

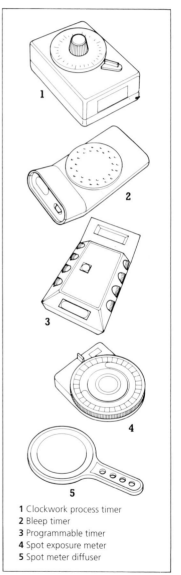

1 Clockwork process timer
2 Bleep timer
3 Programmable timer
4 Spot exposure meter
5 Spot meter diffuser

# Colour Printing Aids

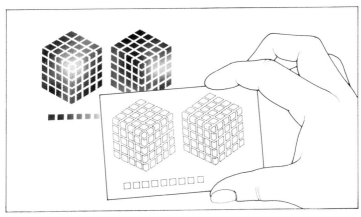

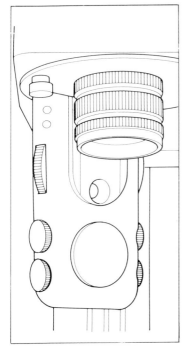

▲ Colour mosaics are the cheapest and simplest form of colour printing aid. With the image diffused completely, a test print is made through a mosaic of different coloured filters. When the print is processed, you look for the square closest to a neutral grey to find the filtration.

▼ Colour analysing meters save you the time and expense of making test prints. Some measure the overall colour of the print and 'integrate to grey' to give the correct colour filtration for the negative. The more expensive meters take a 'spot' colour reading, giving you the information you need for accurate colour, but buying an analyser is no substitute for understanding filtration.

▲ Some colour analysers have a wide range of functions. The model shown above is part of a colour printing system that involves a set of special effects filters as well as an analyser. The analyser itself is attached to a special lens and a probe between the lens elements ensures an integrated colour and density reading of the negative.

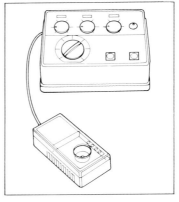

# Print Washers

All prints made by conventional techniques need thorough washing after processing to remove all traces of residual chemicals, but the washing system you need depends on the type of paper that you use. Traditional fibre-based papers absorb large quantities of chemicals and these must be soaked out slowly. Resin-coated (RC) papers, on the other hand, need only rapid surface washing in a stream of water to disperse the unwanted chemicals.

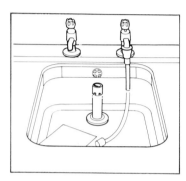

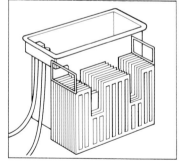

▲ The simplest and cheapest print washer is an overflow pipe that replaces the plug in an ordinary sink, allowing water to drain but keeping it at a constant level. The system is slow but fine for fibre-based prints. The drawbacks are that it prevents you using the sink for other tasks and allows you to wash only a few prints at once.

▲ High-speed washers are designed to make the most of the rapid processing qualities of RC paper, allowing water to flow rapidly over both surfaces of the print. They can wash four prints in less than three minutes, peg separators keeping the prints from overlapping. You can wash fibre prints too, but the flow must be very slow indeed.

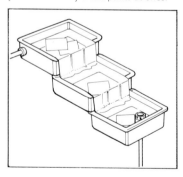

▲ To wash fibre-based prints more efficiently, you can set up a cascade washer with print trays in a bath. Clean water cascades from the top tray to the bottom, while you progressively move each print up through the trays to increasingly fresh water. Six or more prints can be washed at once.

▲ Autowashers are not cheap but are suitable for all types of paper, and take 12 large prints at once. Inflowing water rocks the cradle, ensuring thorough washing, and the compact design means that the autowasher fits neatly on the darkroom draining board, or in a sink, with room to spare.

# Print Dryers

You can dry prints by laying them flat on blotting paper, by hanging them to dry, or even with a hair dryer. If you want to dry large numbers of prints in a hurry, it is worth investing in a proper print dryer. Print dryers may also give a better finish. Unfortunately, not all dryers are suitable for both fibre-based and resin-coated papers. RC papers cannot be dried in rotary or flat-bed glazers, while fibre-based prints tend to curl in hot air dryers.

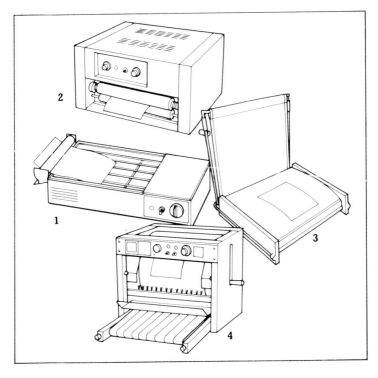

**1** Manual dryer
**2** Auto dryer

**3** Flat-bed glazer
**4** Rotary glazer

● **Manual dryers** blow hot air over the print. Temperature is controlled by a thermostat, but you have to feed the paper through the rollers by hand and take the print off the rack when it is dry.

● **Auto dryers** will take either RC or fibre-based prints straight from the washer – although fibre papers may curl. RC prints are dry in seconds and some dryers can handle 400 prints an hour, but they can be very expensive.

● **Flat-bed glazers** give fibre-based prints a glazed or matt finish and ensure that they dry without curling. The design is simple: the prints are held on a warm curved metal surface by taut canvas. Flat-bed glazers are relatively inexpensive but they can dry fewer than 30 10 x 8in prints an hour.

● **Rotary glazers** can dry hundreds of fibre-based prints an hour, but they are generally too expensive for amateur use.

# Prepare to Process

Black-and-white film processing is easy to master and requires only the barest minimum of special equipment. You do not even need to use a dedicated darkroom, just to have somewhere dark where you canload the film into the tank. Only by processing films yourself can you achieve the level of consistency and control over negatives needed for high-quality black-and-white prints.

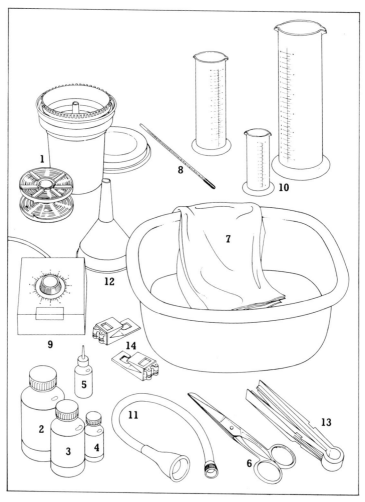

**What you need**

1 Film processing tank
2 Developer
3 Stop bath
4 Fixer
5 Wetting agent
6 Scissors
7 Absorbent cloths

8 Thermometer
9 Timer or watch with second hand
10 Graduates
11 Washing tube
12 Funnel
13 Squeegee
14 Film clips

**Process steps**
- **In darkness**
1 Load the film into the tank

- **In daylight**
2 Prepare the chemicals
3 Develop the film
4 Rinse in stop bath
5 Fix the film
6 Wash
7 Dry

- **A processing tank** is the one item of equipment for which there is no real substitute. To keep the cost of chemicals down, use the smallest tank you can, or save up exposed films for processing in a single batch.

- **Never try to estimate** – always make accurate measurements or consistent results will be impossible.

- **Use a timer** to time process steps. Although a watch with a second hand is quite accurate enough for black-and-white film processing, processing times are so long that it is easy to lose track of how many minutes have passed. A timer solves this problem. If you do use a watch, write down the finishing time as soon as you begin each step.

- **Beware of pointed scissors:** they can scratch the film as you are cutting it in the dark. Snub-nosed scissors are a much safer bet.

- **Use a 'universal' developer** suitable for all black-and-white films (and prints as well) for your first experiments in film processing. Only graduate to the more specialized developers (see pages 40–41) once you can achieve completely consistent results with the simpler processes.

- **A stop bath** between developing and fixing is not vital. Thorough rinsing in tap water is usually enough to prevent carry-over of developer to the fixing stage, but a proper stop bath neutralizes the action of the developer instantly, giving much more accurate control over development time.

- **Fixer can be reused** a number of times, so have a suitable brown glass bottle handy to store it (clear and green glass let too much light in).

- **Do not use detergent** as a substitute for a 'wetting agent', no matter what anyone tells you. Modern detergents are far too harsh and contain additives that leave smears on the film. Some new detergents may cause pitting of the film surface, which can be irreparable.

- **Warming chemicals**. To work properly, the processing solutions must be held at a constant 20°C (68°F). If you have no tempering box (see page 17), the best way to keep the solutions at the right temperature is to stand the containers in a trough of warm water until the moment they are to be used.

- **Warming the bath**. To bring the water bath to the process temperature, start with the water slightly cooler and gradually add hot water, checking the temperature all the time. This is much easier than adding cold water to bring the temperature down.

- **Label the solutions** in the order that they are to be used, and arrange them in order across the trough so that they fall easily to hand.

# Load the Film

To load the film into the tank, you need complete darkness, although you can perform every other processing stage in broad daylight. A proper darkroom is by far the best place to work, but anywhere that can be made securely light-proof will do.

If you plan to process films often but have no darkroom, think about investing in a changing bag, which is a special light-proof bag with armholes. For occasional forays, though, try loading the film in a wardrobe, in a cupboard under the stairs or even under the bedclothes. But check that it is genuinely light-proof, and bear in mind that it takes at least ten minutes for your eyes to adjust to the dark. To be safe, process films only at night.

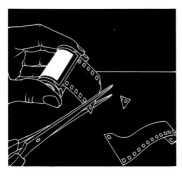

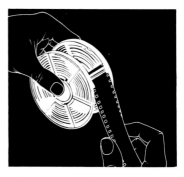

**Self-loading spiral**
**1** In complete darkness, remove the film from its light-proof cassette and cup the spool in the palm of your left hand. Cut off the film end between perforations and cut off the corners to make the film easier to load.

**2** Transfer the spool to your right hand. Then, with the left, hold the spiral vertically so that the lugs at the start of the spiral are at the top. Holding the spool firmly, and the film end between thumb and forefinger, gently feed the film under the lugs until it catches.

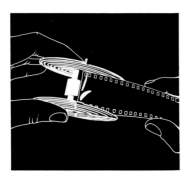

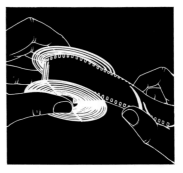

**Centre-loading spiral**
**1** Stainless steel spirals are loaded from the centre out. In darkness, open the spool and cut off the film end, as with plastic spirals. Then, arching the film in between thumb and forefinger, guide the end towards the hub of the spiral.

**2** Attach the film to the hub either by pushing it under the spring clip or hooking it on the lugs, depending which is used. Then, with your right hand, gently draw out about 15cm (6in) of film from the spool, while holding the spiral firmly in your left hand.

● **Practise loading the spiral** in daylight with an old roll of film. Practise first with your eyes open, then, once you have mastered that, with them shut.

● **Clean and dry the spiral** well before you load the film – any trace of moisture will make the film stick.

● **Steel spirals** can be dried by warming briefly in a low oven. DO NOT try this with plastic spirals.

● **Keep a light-proof bag** – a heavy black rubbish bag will do. If anything goes wrong, you can put everything in the bag and stop for a breather.

● **Lay out all you need** so that it falls easily to hand in the dark.

● **Open film cassettes** (in the dark) with a bottle opener if they have staples around the spool. If not, tap the end on the table.

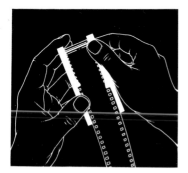

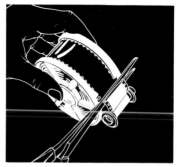

**3** Once the film is slotted smoothly beneath the lugs, operate the self-load mechanism by turning the two sides of the spiral alternately to and fro. If the film sticks, wiggle it sideways a little or pull the film back out a little way and start again. Never force the film.

**4** When all the film is in the spiral, snip off the spool and tape down the loose film end. Then drop the spiral gently into the tank, fit all the components, including locking collar and spindle, and screw or push the lid down firmly. You are now ready to start processing.

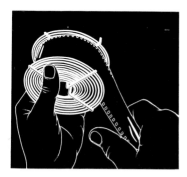

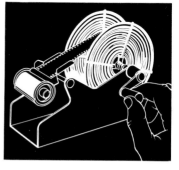

**3** To take up the free length of film, turn the spiral smoothly with your left hand, keeping the film and the spiral aligned. As you turn the spiral, make sure the film is taken up. Repeat this motion until all the film is on the spiral and then cut off the spool.

**4** With a reel-loader, loading the spiral could not be simpler, although as with hand-loading, practice is vital. Remember not to rewind the film end right back into the cassette. With a little film protruding you can set the loader up in normal lighting.

# Develop and Fix

Once the film is loaded safely into the tank, you can turn on the lights and start the processing sequence. Every darkroom worker knows just how important it is to control the process times and temperatures carefully. But I have always found that consistent technique can be just as important. The only way to achieve high-quality results, and repeat them again and again, is to follow the same processing routine meticulously. If, for example, you start timing development the moment you pour developer into the tank, always do so. This way you can make minute adjustments and gradually refine your technique. Different films require different processing routines, and it pays to master one film/developer combination before trying others.

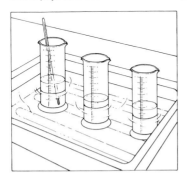

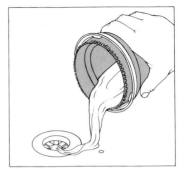

**1** Before you start to develop the film, clean the thermometer thoroughly and check the temperature of the developer. If it has fallen below 20°C (68°F), add a little hot water to the water bath to raise the temperature again. Clean the thermometer after use.

**2** To start development, hold the tank at a 45° angle and pour the measured developer into the tank mouth. Pour the solution as quickly as possible, but keep the flow smooth – any air bubbles may cause uneven development. Once all the developer is in, start timing.

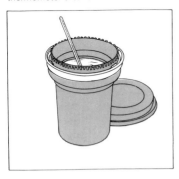

**5** Towards the end of the recommended development period, check the temperature of the developer in the tank. If the temperature has dropped more than 1.5°C (3°F), extend the development time according to the manufacturers' instructions.

**6** Start to pour the developer away ten seconds before development is completed – development will continue until you pour in the stop bath. Once the tank is empty, immediately fill the tank with stop solution, or clean water, and agitate for one minute.

● **Do not pre-soak** ordinary black-and-white film in warm water before development. Modern developers contain wetting agents which prevent air bubbles. Chromogenic films do need pre-soaking, otherwise the coolness of the film will bring the temperature below that needed for processing, thus causing underdevelopment.

● **Stand the tank** in the water bath for a few minutes before pouring in the developer. This should bring the tank up to the process temperature.

● **Always agitate** in the same way to ensure consistent, predictable results.

● **Fix fast films slightly longer** – the emulsions often contain silver iodide which is less easily removed.

● **A milky sheen** to the film after fixing indicates exhausted fixer.

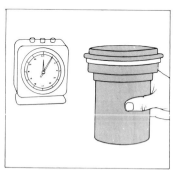

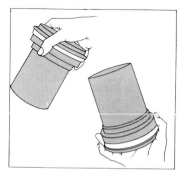

**3** Immediately the tank is filled, push the lid on firmly and, with the tank upright, tap the base sharply on the bench. This should dislodge any air bubbles that may be trapped on the film. Repeat this trick every time you pour a new solution into the tank.

**4** Agitate thoroughly during development. If your tank does not leak when turned upside down (test it beforehand) agitate by inverting the tank once every 20 seconds. If it leaks, agitate vigorously with the twiddle stick for five seconds every 20 seconds.

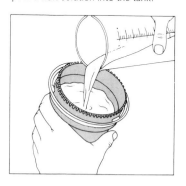

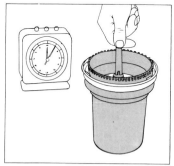

**7** Pour away the stop bath and fill the tank with fixer. Take care not to use exhausted fixer, though, or the film may well be discoloured. Once the tank is full, rap it sharply on the bench to dislodge air bubbles, and start to agitate immediately.

**8** Agitate continuously for the first 30 seconds and, thereafter, for five seconds (or two inversions) every 30 seconds. At the end of the recommended fixing period, pour the fixer through a funnel into a storage bottle for use again at a later date.

# Wash and Dry

With developing and fixing complete, it is tempting to rush through the final processing stages to see your pictures. But meticulous care is as crucial in washing and drying as at any other stage. Traces of unwanted chemicals left by inadequate washing can easily stain the film or cut short the life of the negative. Careless drying can leave blemishes on the film that no amount of retouching on the print can disguise.

You can wash film in either running water or half-a-dozen changes of water. I usually use running water, because it is less trouble. But changes of water clean the film just as well, as long as you shake the tank vigorously. Recommended washing times vary, but 30 minutes is usually enough.

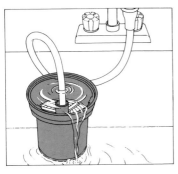

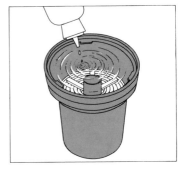

**1** Stand the tank in a sink to wash the film. The best method is to direct tap water right into the bottom of the tank through a hose. If you have no hose, stand the tank open beneath the tap but empty the tank and turn over the spiral frequently.

**2** Once the film is washed, fill the tank with fresh water. To ensure even drying, add a little wetting agent. For each 200ml of water, you need 10ml of wetting agent stock solution, made up by diluting a bottle of wetting agent with nine parts of water.

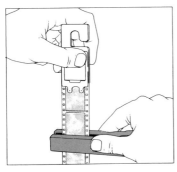

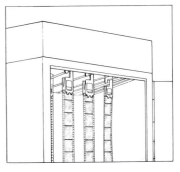

**4** Gently pull on the film clip to withdraw the film from the spiral. Clean the blades of a squeegee to remove any minute grit particles. Then, in a continuous stroke, run the squeegee down the film to remove all the excess water from the surface.

**5** Hang the film to dry in a totally dust-free environment, preferably a proper drying cabinet. If you have problems with dust, spray the drying area with water from a garden plant spray, and keep the area fairly warm to dry the film as quickly as possible.

● **Film technology** is such that reticulation (where warm, wet film looks like crazy paving) is now very rare.

● **When you use a hardening fixer,** wash the film for twice as long.

● **Cut short washing time** when you need the film urgently by using a hypo clearing agent, followed by a brief wash in clean water.

● **Speed up drying** with a final rinse in ethyl alcohol diluted with ten per cent water.

● **In hard water areas,** wipe down the film especially carefully to prevent white drying marks. If the water is exceptionally hard, give a final rinse in distilled water. Alternatively, a supply of filtered water in the darkroom will eliminate the problem.

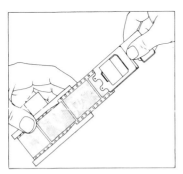

**3** After the final rinse, gently shake the spiral to remove excess water. Then, with the film still in the spiral, attach a film clip to the outer end of the film. At this stage, the film is very easily damaged and the film clip makes it easier to handle safely.

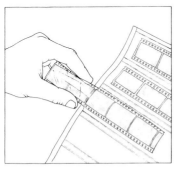

**6** Once the film is dry, cut into strips six frames long (if they are any shorter than this they will be awkward to handle without damaging them). Slide the strips immediately into protective sleeves made from acid-free paper.

### Process chromogenic films

Ilford's XP2 black-and-white film forms the image with coloured dyes rather than particles of silver. This 'chromogenic' or dye-image film is processed in a different way to conventional black-and-white film, resembling more closely colour film processing (see page 68). As with colour films, the fixing bath for XP2 film includes chemicals that bleach away all the silver, leaving only the dye image. Similarly, for the developer to work properly, process temperatures must be high and accurately controlled.

**1** Load the film into the tank.

**2** Pre-soak by filling the tank with warm water at 40°C (104°F). Empty after one minute.

**3** Develop for five minutes at 38°C (100°F), inverting the tank four times in the first 10 seconds of each minute.

**4** Bleach/fix for five minutes at 38°C (100°F), inverting the tank four times in the first 10 seconds of each minute.

**5** Wash in six changes of water warmed to 38°C (100°F).

**6** Dry as conventional black-and-white film.

# Assess the Negative

After each film is processed and dried, take a critical look at the negatives. If there are no obvious faults, such as totally blank frames or double exposures, examine the film frame by frame through a magnifier. Minor errors in exposure and processing may be hardly noticeable at first, yet they can take that edge off your prints. Unless you make this close examination you can easily go on printing sub-standard negatives without appreciating why you can never achieve quite the same sparkle that the professionals manage. If you want perfect prints, strive for perfection in your negatives.

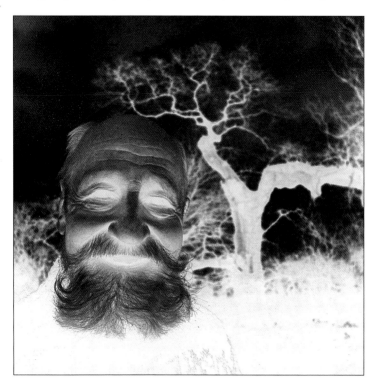

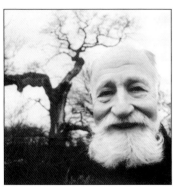

A good negative shows a full range of tones from dark to light. Detail is clearly visible in both shadows (clear areas) and highlights (dark areas). The deepest shadows in the picture are as clear as the unexposed film edges but the highlights are nowhere too dense to read type through. There is also a good range of mid-tones. Look for mid-grey edge markings on the film too. If your negatives show all these qualities, they should enlarge well and give rich prints.

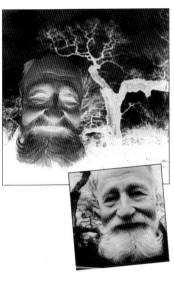

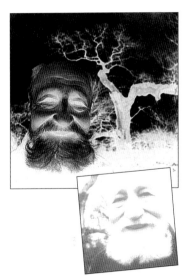

An underexposed negative gives a dark but lifeless print with poor shadow detail and contrast. The negative looks pale and thin even in the highlights while the film edge markings are normal.

An overexposed negative gives a light and flat print with poor highlight detail. The negative is dark and dense even though both the contrast range and the edge markings look normal.

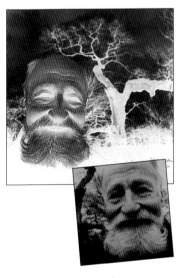

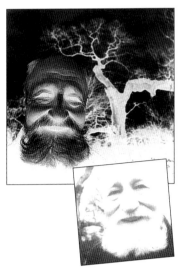

An underdeveloped negative gives a soft, low-contrast print. The negative is thin and grey and the range of tones is limited. The chief symptom, though, is the appeerance of pale and weak edge markings on the film.

An overdeveloped negative gives an excessively contrasty print with few mid-tones. The negative has very dense highlights but fairly thin shadows. The sign here is very dark film edge markings.

# Exploit Developers

Standard developers give a compromise between film speed, grain and contrast that works well for most pictures. But sometimes you need to emphasize one of these characteristics to achieve a particular effect. This is where alternative developers and processing routines come into their own.

● **Use a fine-grain developer** like Kodak XTOL or Ilford ID-11 for most of your routine work. They keep visible clumping of film grains to a minimum without affecting film speed noticeably.

● **Develop films** for giant prints in extra fine-grain developer like Perceptol and adjust the camera exposure. Perceptol cuts film speed by one stop.

● **Gain film speed,** when the film has to be underexposed, by using a speed-increasing developer. Some of these, such as Ilford's Microphen, allow you to expose the film two or three stops less than the nominal film speed. Grain is increased slightly.

● **Make pictures look sharp** by using a high acutance developer. High acutance developers create an illusion of sharpness by emphasizing any edges that appear in the picture. Where a dark area meets a light area, the developer will exaggerate the difference in tone, giving a dark outline to the dark area and a light outline to the light area.

● **Do not use acutance developers** with films faster than ISO 200. The increased grain size will negate the acutance effect.

● **Increase contrast** by extending the development time.

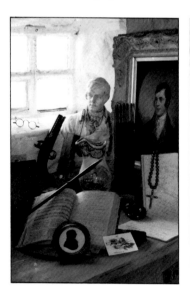

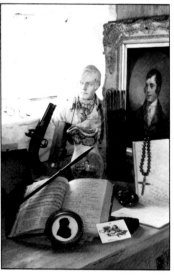

▲ Low contrast developers, like fine-grain developers, work by stopping individual silver grains from forming clumps. When used with slow films, which tend towards high contrast, fine-grain developers give negatives of normal contrast.

▲ General-purpose developers, have moderate alkalinity and provide a reasonable compromise for all types of black-and-white materials, giving a good tonal range and fairly fine grain while retaining detail in both shadows and highlights.

## Push processing

If you shoot in light too dim to give the shutter speed or depth of field your film needs, try 'uprating' it – exposing as if the film is faster than its ISO rating. Compensate for this underexposure by increasing development time. This is called 'push processing'.

● **Do not push process** unless absolutely necessary. It increases grain and contrast dramatically.

● **Think in aperture stops** when uprating; it is easier than using film speeds. Doubling the film speed means you can give one stop less exposure.●

**Extend development** by roughly 40 per cent for each stop you cut exposure if in doubt. Otherwise follow the directions given by the makers. Keep standard times for chromogenic film.

● **Never push** more than three stops. Push processing not only increases grain and contrast, but also increases 'development fog'. The gain in contrast initially offsets this, but beyond three stops fog overwhelms all shadow detail.

● **Use a speed-increasing developer** such as Microphen. This will boost shadow development at the expense of highlights, so compensating for the gain in contrast when pushing.

● **Use two-bath** developer for big increases in film speed. The first bath develops highlights but is exhausted fast. The second develops shadows.

● **Try clip tests** with important films. This means clipping the end off the films and processing at various times to find the time that gives best results with each roll of exposed film.

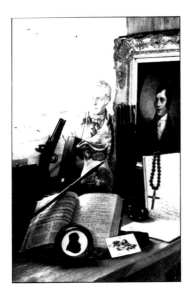

▲ High-contrast developers are very highly alkaline. They produce negatives with dense highlights and thin shadows. This degree of contrast is not usually needed in normal negatives, and HC developers are usually meant only for line and lith film.

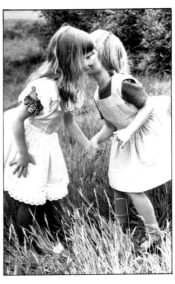

▲ High-acutance developers give an illusion of sharpness. They help to retain detail by concentrating development near the surface of the emulsion and by increasing edge contrast in the negative. They work best with films slower than ISO 200.

# Prepare to Print

The print is the culmination of the long process that begins when you first frame the subject in the viewfinder, and it is worth taking great pains to achieve the finest quality you can. Remember, people judge the photograph by the print, as well as the original idea. No one will appreciate the subtle gradations of light if the print is muddy and flat. To get an idea of the quality possible, try to see the work of master printers like Ansel Adams, not in reproduction but as photographic prints. Adams regarded the print as a vital part of the creation of a photograph: if 'the negative is the score … the print is the performance.'

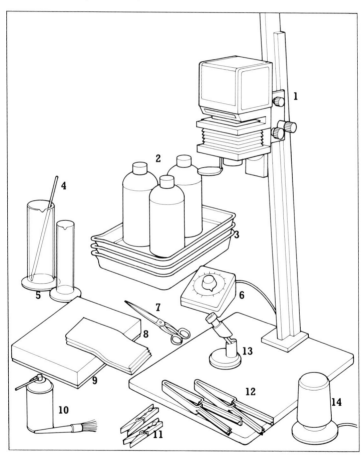

**What you need**

1. Enlarger
2. Developer, fixer and stop
3. Three processing trays
4. Spirit thermometer
5. Graduates, one large, one small
6. Exposure timer
7. Scissors
8. Absorbent cloths
9. Print paper
10. Dust removers
11. Clothes pegs
12. Print squeegees
13. Magnifying focus finder
14. Safelight

## Making a print

**1** Make a contact sheet
**2** Choose the negative
**3** Compose the image
**4** Select the paper
**5** Set up the enlarger
**6** Test for exposure
**7** Expose the print
**8** Process the print

● **The darkroom** need only be big enough to contain the enlarger and a surface for three processing trays. If need be, you can carry the print to the kitchen for washing. If you do wash prints outside the darkroom, though, remember not to open the darkroom door while unfixed paper is lying on the bench, and use a spare tray to carry the dripping print.

● **Match safelight and print paper** for maximum light in the darkroom. Most print papers can be safely handled in a fairly bright amber light. The traditional, much dimmer red light is only needed for working with lith film. Correctly filtered sodium lamps can be used in colour print processing, but are expensive. Some variable contrast papers may be fogged by the amber light, however, so check the maker's recommendations.

● **Cheap acrylic safelights** are not always totally safe. Check their safeness as below, and leave paper exposed for the minimum time.

● **Check your safelight** by exposing paper under the enlarger with an exposure long enough to give a light grey print. But before processing the print, leave a coin on the exposed paper for two minutes under the safelight. If the outline of the coin is visible on the paper after processing, the safelight is not safe.

● **Keep the darkroom at 20°C** (68°F) as nearly as you can. This is the best way to maintain the chemicals in the open trays at the right temperature so that they do not deteriorate.

## Dealing with dust

● **Beware of dust** when printing: it ruins more prints than virtually any other single fault. Keep the darkroom as clean as possible at all times.

● **Clean with a vacuum cleaner** rather than a brush or duster. A brush will simply lift dust into the air, rather than removing it.

● **Wear white, lint-free gloves** when handling dry negatives to avoid leaving greasy fingerprints on the film.

● **Mix chemicals outside** the darkroom, especially if you are working with powders.

● **Wipe surfaces regularly** with a damp cloth.

● **Do not use a fan heater** to keep the room warm; a bar heater stirs up much less dust.

● **Clean each negative** carefully with an anti-static blower brush before printing.

● **Put the negative away** as soon as you finish printing.

● **Use a glassless negative carrier** in the enlarger, or at least one with a single glass, when printing from 35mm or smaller negatives. Glass surfaces attract dust and in a double glass carrier there are four surfaces to attract dust. But if you use a glassless carrier, keep exposures brief or the negative will curl. Glassless negative holders do, however, crop more of the image than glass carriers.

# Process the Print

One of the attractions of black-and-white printing is that you can watch the print right through the processing sequence. In particular, you can assess the image as it appears in the developing bath and control this process accordingly. Modern high-speed developers, in combination with RC papers, have cut developing times so much that the chances for manipulation are considerably less than they used to be. But you may still be able to rescue a slightly overexposed print, for instance, by cutting short development, or boost contrast in an underexposed print by extending development. Before you try to experiment with alternative processing routines, though, be sure that you can achieve consistent results with the standard routine.

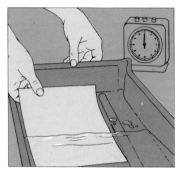

**1** Prepare for processing by filling the trays with developer, stop and fixer to a depth of about 2 cm (¾in). To start processing, raise one end of the developing tray about 4cm (1½in), then quickly slide the exposed print, face up, into the shallow end.

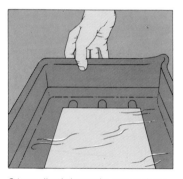

**2** Immediately lower the tray so that a wave of developer completely covers the print. Start timing development. With a high-speed developer, the image should start to appear after about six seconds. Move the print around continuously.

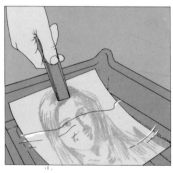

**5** Lower the print, face up, into the fixer and agitate by rocking the tray gently for the first 15–20 seconds. Be sure that all the print is constantly covered in fixer. After one minute (five for fibre-based prints), it is safe to switch on normal white light.

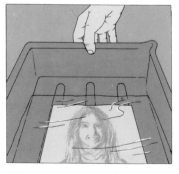

**6** Rock the tray occasionally until the recommended fixing time is up. With RC papers, fixing time can be two minutes or even less with combinations such as Ilfospeed paper and Hypam fixer. Fibre-based papers must usually be fixed for ten minutes.

● **Stick to makers' process times** unless you have a very good reason for variation. Only the recommended process times will give optimum results.

● **If you vary development** by eye, remember that prints look darker and more contrasty by safelight than daylight, and are best judged when dry.

● **Keep solutions at 20°C (68°F)** as near as possible, by standing the tray in warm water or, better, on a thermostatically controlled tray warmer. There is some margin for error with black-and-white print processing – it speeds up if the developer is too hot (up to a point), and slows down if it is too cold. Keeping temperatures near 20°C (68°F) ensures consistent results.

● **Dry test prints** more quickly by blowing them with a hair dryer, as a few watermarks will not matter.

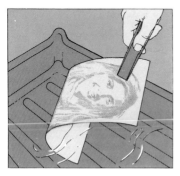

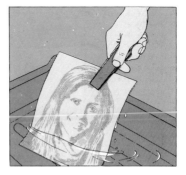

**3** Once the image begins to appear, turn the print over, and leave face down until the last third of development time. Then, turn it face up and continue to agitate. When development is complete lift the print and allow the developer to drain away for a few seconds.

**4** Once development is complete, lower the print into the stop bath. With RC papers, this bath can be water; with traditional fibre-based papers you need an acid stop bath. Rock the tray of stop bath for about 30 seconds, then lift the print and let it drain briefly.

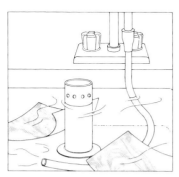

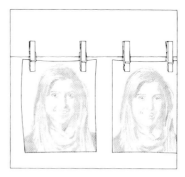

**7** Wash the print in running water for four minutes (30 minutes for fibre-based papers). But be careful that prints do not stick together in the sink. Keep the water at a temperature of between 20–25°C (70–75°F) or use five changes of warm water instead.

**8** Wipe the excess water from the print surface with a print squeegee in a single continuous stroke. Then dry the print either by hanging it up, or by laying it flat on a sheet of newspaper or in a drying rack. Fibre-based papers take much longer to dry than RC.

**45**

# Make a Contact Proof

To help decide which negatives to print, I always make a contact proof from every film. A contact proof is simply a positive print of all the frames on the film, made by exposing the whole film in contact with a single sheet of print paper. It provides not only a wealth of information to guide you when you make an enlargement, but also an easy-to-file source of reference for every one of your pictures. Cut into strips of six frames, a full 36-exposure roll of 35mm film fits neatly onto a 10 x 8in sheet.

Contact proofs are easy to make. All you need, besides a darkroom and print processing materials, are a controllable light source to expose the print and a sheet of glass to hold the negatives firmly against the print paper.

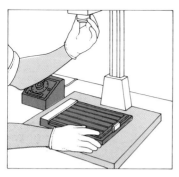

**1** Before making your first contact proof, you must work out the exposure needed. To do this, place the contact frame or glass on the enlarger baseboard. Switch on the enlarger light, and move the head until the light fully covers the frame. Stop the lens down to *f*11.

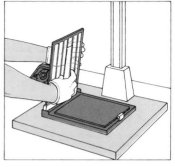

**2** To make the test, place a strip of clear film from a film end under the centre of the glass. Switch on the safelight and turn off the room and enlarger light. Take a sheet of print paper from its packet and cut off a small strip. Place the rest of the sheet in the packet and reseal.

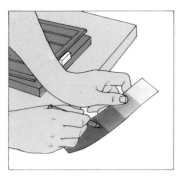

**5** Once the test strip is ready, examine it in normal room lighting. The strip should have a series of grey bands. Find the first band that gives a full black (next to a dark grey band) and work out how long this band was exposed for. This is the correct proof exposure.

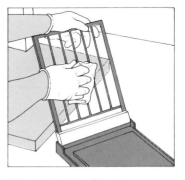

**6** Clean both sides of the glass very carefully using a blower brush and an antistatic cloth. Take the negatives you wish to proof from their storage sleeves. Gently clean off fingerprints and drying marks from the shiny side of the film with a soft, lint-free cloth.

- **Mark the height** of the enlarger head on the column when you make your test exposure, or measure the height of the head and write it down. You can then set the head at the same height again, and use the exposure established by your test for all proofs from the same film type.

- **If you have no enlarger**, try exposing with a desk lamp held at various heights above the print.

- **Use a contact frame** if you make many proofs. They align the negatives neatly and space them so that the negative numbers are recorded.

- **Use grade 2 paper** to give a good indication of the tonal range you can expect in enlargements.

- **If every test band is black**, you have exposed for too long. Repeat the test with shorter exposure times.

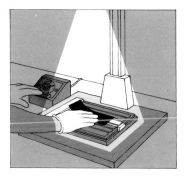

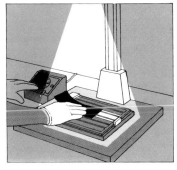

**3** Place the paper under the clear film, and cover four-fifths of it with opaque card. Switch on the enlarger light and start timing. After five seconds (this will depend on the enlargement factor and the brightness of the lighting system) uncover a further fifth of the strip.

**4** Continue to uncover successive fifths of the strip every five seconds, until the entire strip has been exposed. Switch off the enlarger and remove the strip of paper from under the glass. Still under safelight, process, wash and dry the print normally.

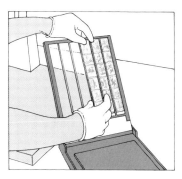

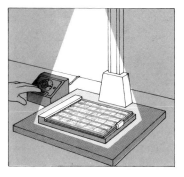

**7** Carefully slide the negatives into the tracks on the frame, taking care to handle only the edges of the film. Keep the shiny side of the film up against the glass. If you are using a plain sheet of glass, lay the negatives on print paper under safelight.

**8** Under safelight again, take out a full sheet of print paper and lay it, shiny side up, in the contact frame. Lock the glass cover in place. Switch on the enlarger to make the tested exposure. Process normally. With plain glass, lay the glass over the paper and negatives.

# Use the Contact Proof

A good contact proof shows at a glance which images are not worth printing up. But close inspection through a magnifying loupe can actually reveal much more. You can see if images are critically sharp; if detail is present in both highlights and shadows; if pictures suffer from unwanted distractions; and so on. You can also see clearly which pictures work and which do not, and if any can be improved by close cropping.

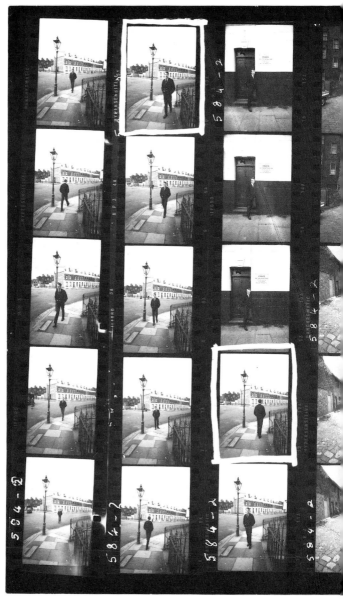

● **Make a contact proof** work. Use it to gain all the information you need to make the best print from each negative.

● **Use an old slide mount** or, better, a magnifying loupe, to view each frame, undistracted by the frames.

● **Mark up the contact proof** with wax or 'chinagraph' pencils. Ring the images you wish to use.

● **Decide how to crop** each frame with a pair of opposing L-shaped cards. Mark the crop on the proof.

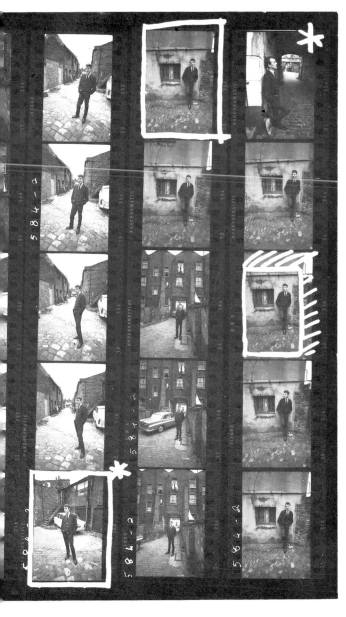

# Choose the Paper Grade

To make the most of your pictures, you need to match carefully each negative and the paper you print it on. Print paper comes in a range of different contrast grades, usually numbered from 0 to 5, but, ideally, you would print all your negatives on Grade 2 or 3 paper, except when you want a special effect. Grades 2 and 3 give a print with a good range of tones from a perfectly exposed, perfectly developed negative with an average range of densities. On Grade 4 or 5 paper, such a negative gives a hard, contrasty print with a lack of mid tones; on Grade 0 or 1, the print is soft and flat. However, because many negatives are inevitably imperfectly exposed or developed, and many subjects do not have an average range of densities you must often use the more extreme paper grades to get good prints.

In choosing paper grades, I usually aim to achieve a range of tones matching that in a print from an average negative on Grade 2 or 3 paper. So I print a soft, flat negative on hard Grade 4 or 5 paper, and a hard contrasty negative on soft Grade 0 or 1 paper.

● **Standardize on one grade** of paper and try to make all your negatives match this paper. Grade 2 is an ideal standard grade.

● **Different brands of paper** may give different contrast characteristics for the same paper grade.

● **Never change brands** for different grades; the difference in performance will be too great for consistent results.

● **Use a soft grade of paper** for contact proofs and work-prints for important prints. Only a soft print will reveal textures and tonal differences in all of the negative.

● **Print one grade harder** than ideal then burn in and dodge missing details and tones. This will give a punchier print than the correct grade.

● **Print underdeveloped negatives** on Grade 4 or 5 to maximize contrast.

● **Print overdeveloped negatives** on soft Grade 0 or 1 paper to bring out the mid tones correctly.

● **Variable contrast papers** (eg, Agfa Multicontrast and Ilford Multigrade IV) have come on in leaps and bounds. Some now offer Grade 00 (softer even than Grade 0) to a true Grade 5.

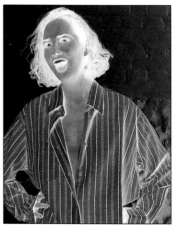

▲ Prints on various grades of paper from the negative above. The negative is well exposed and developed and has a good range of tones. Printed on Grade 0 or Grade 1 paper, the full range of tones and detail is retained. But there are few deep blacks and few bright highlights – even the girl's pale shirt is slightly grey. The overall effect is muddy and flat. The negative prints well on both Grade 2 and 3 paper, but the softer Grade 2 print is better because the scene is fairly contrasty. On Grade 4 paper, shadows are deep and highlights poor but detail is disappearing. On Grade 5, mid tones, as well as shadow and highlight detail, are lost almost completely.

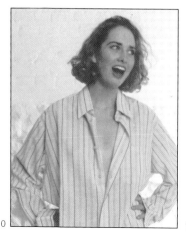

0

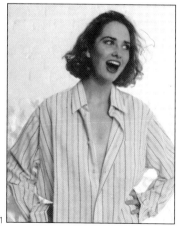

1

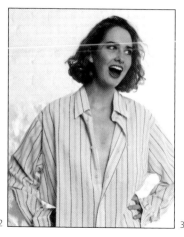

2

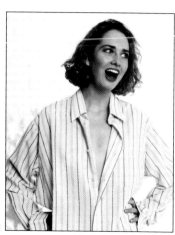

3

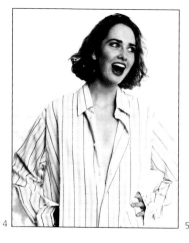

4

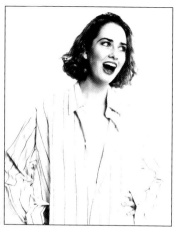

5

# Prepare to Enlarge

When making prints, careful preparation of the enlarger is surprisingly important. Slight errors in focusing, small specks of dust on the negative and inaccurate cropping can all take the edge off otherwise good prints. Dust on the negative is a particularly common problem. Remember, a small speck of dust will be enlarged on the print as much as the negative itself. Extra care in setting up the enlarger will be well rewarded in the final print.

In choosing what size to make your enlargement, do not be tempted to try unreasonably large prints. Big prints certainly have extra visual impact, but they are expensive to make and magnify all deficiencies. To make giant prints from 35mm negatives, you need quality equipment and superb technique.

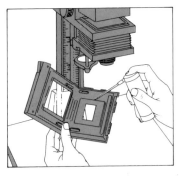

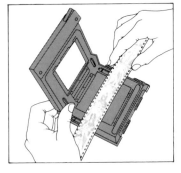

**1** To prepare to enlarge, first clean the lens carefully with a soft brush and a piece of tissue. Then remove the negative carrier and dust it with a blower brush or a jet of compressed air. With glass negative carriers, carefully wipe off any fingermarks.

**2** Hold the chosen negative obliquely in the enlarger beam to check for dust spots. Flick dust off with a soft brush; if any dust clings to the film, try using an antistatic pistol. Then lay the negative in the carrier so that all the frame you wish to print is visible.

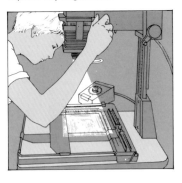

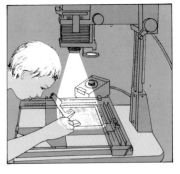

**5** Adjust the focus control on the enlarger head until the image on the easel appears perfectly sharp. As you adjust the focus, the image size may change a little. If so, gradually raise or lower the enlarger head until the image is the correct size once more.

**6** Now fine tune the focus, preferably with a focus magnifier. With a focus magnifier you must have a sheet of print paper on the easel to ensure the image is in the right plane. Use the grain pattern to focus. Chromogenic film has no grain, so focus on fine detail.

● **Be prepared to crop 35mm images**, or accept a little wasted paper. Surprisingly, there is no standard paper size to match the 35mm format, although A4 is better than 10 x 8in.

● **Consider perspective.** Theoretically, correct perspective is achieved only when the print size and viewing distance correspond with the focal length of the picture-taking lens. Thus,

with the standard 50mm lens for 35mm, only a 5 x 8in print gives correct perspective when viewed from 25cm (10in). Bear in mind that, except for special effect, prints of shots with long lenses should be smaller, or viewed from further away, than prints of wide-angle shots. Similarly, prints to be mounted in a confined space, such as a hall, should be smaller than prints to be displayed in a large room.

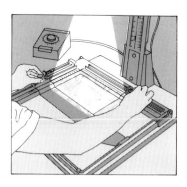

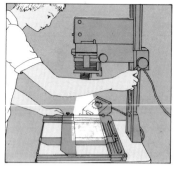

**3** Replace the negative carrier in the enlarger and check that it is properly in position. Adjust the masks on the easel until they give the print size you have chosen. Centre the frame under the enlarger, turn off the room lights and switch on the enlarger.

**4** Open the enlarger lens to its maximum aperture to give the brightest possible image. Focus the image roughly, then slowly raise or lower the enlarger head – usually by turning the crank on the column – until the image exactly fits the frame on the easel.

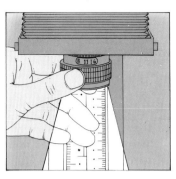

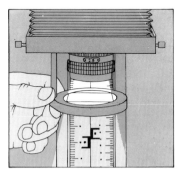

**7** Close the enlarger lens down at least two stops below its maximum aperture to ensure the image is as sharp as possible. As you change the aperture, the focus may shift slightly on some enlargers. If so, quickly run through the focusing procedure again.

**8** Once the image is perfectly sharp, remove the sheet of paper from the easel, being careful not to jog it at all. Then very gently swing the red filter across beneath the lens. You cannot use the red filter with VC papers, as the light will still fog the paper to a degree.

# Test for Exposure

Once the enlarger is set up and focused, you need to work out just what exposure the negative requires. An experienced printer can often guess the exposure from the brightness of the image on the baseboard and then adjust for any error by watching the print in the developer. The less experienced must rely on test strips and exposure meters.

Test strips seem tedious and use a great deal of expensive paper, but they are really the only completely reliable way of establishing exposure. The correct exposure is the exposure you want; a meter can only give an average exposure. Only a test strip arms you with the information that you need to give the exposure needed to get the best print from each negative.

● **Make large test strips.** Small strips are a false economy. To give an accurate indication of the exposure, each band must include enough variation of tone to be representative of the whole print.

● **Lay the strip diagonally** across the picture. In landscapes this ensures that the strip includes sky and land.

● **Stop down the aperture** one more setting if exposures of less than five seconds give over-exposed results.

● **Use the same exposure** as indicated by the test strip for all similar prints from the same roll of film. Check the negatives' density to see if the images are similar.

● **Calibrate an exposure meter** by printing a typical negative to give the density you want in your prints. Store the exposure time given for this print in the meter's memory, and it will give prints of similar density for all that batch of paper.

● **Spot meters** need calibrating more carefully than integrating meters.

● **Use a spot meter** to select the correct paper grade by comparing the densities of the shadows and the highlights.

● **Convert your spot meter** to an integrating meter for quickfire prints by holding a sheet of frosted acetate under the enlarger: this will have the effect of diffusing the image.

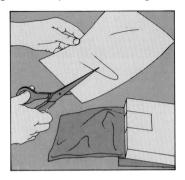

**1** Under safelight, take a sheet of paper from the packet. Then with a sharp pair of scissors, cut a long, broad strip from the sheet. The strip should be at least 5cm (2in) wide, even with 10 x 8in paper. Put the rest of the sheet safely back in the packet and close the box.

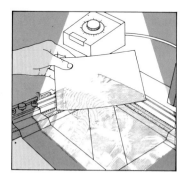

**4** After five seconds, switch off the enlarger. Stop the timer and cover a fifth of the test strip with opaque card, being careful not to move the test strip in the slightest. When the card is in position, switch on the enlarger and start timing again.

● **Simplify exposure tests** by using a step-wedge. This is a sheet of film with windows of varying densities. These densities correspond to various exposure times. To use a step-wedge, you simply lay it over the printing paper and make an exposure. Because of the different film densities, different parts of the print will get different exposure.

● **Expose a wedge for 60 seconds**, unless otherwise specified by the maker.

The number by the window that gives the correct exposure will give the print exposure in seconds.

● **Reduce the exposure** for the step-wedge to fine tune the exposure. Then adjust the exposure times according to those marked on the corresponding windows.

● **Do not use a step-wedge** for difficult or large prints.

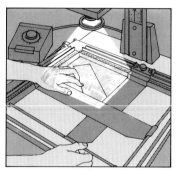

**2** Check that the red filter still covers the lens and switch on the enlarger. Lay the strip of paper on the image so that it shows both dark and light tones. Place a large sheet of opaque card nearby. Turn off the enlarger and swing back the red filter.

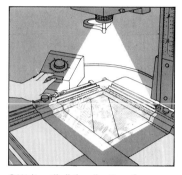

**3** Wait until all the vibrations from moving the red filter have died down. Then switch on the enlarger and start timing. Get a piece of opaque card ready to slide into position for the next stage of the exposure. Keep your eye on the timer all the time.

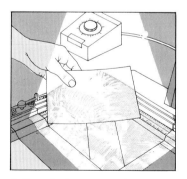

**5** After a further ten seconds, switch off the enlarger and cover a further fifth of the strip. Switch on the enlarger and start timing again. Repeat this procedure after 20 and 40 seconds, covering a further fifth of the card each time, until the whole card is covered.

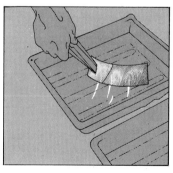

**6** Develop the print for the recommended time, rinse, fix and leave it to dry. When the strip is dry, examine it closely in normal daylight. Work out the exposure time for the best band in the strip. This is your main print exposure, or the base for further tests.

# Make a Print

With the paper chosen and an exposure established, you can make the first full print from the negative. For most photographers, this first full print is also the final print. For many master printers, however, it is only a beginning, one of a series of work-prints that provide all the information needed to create a fine print. Few people can afford to adopt this approach all the time, and the first print should be quite adequate for handing round to family and friends. But if you are producing a print for mounting or for a show, it is worth making a whole series of work-prints, gradually refining the balance of tones at each step. Aim to achieve good deep blacks and brilliant whites at the first step. Then go on to fill in all the subtle mid tones.

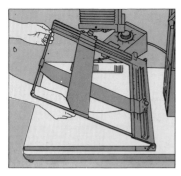

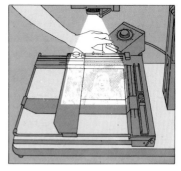

**1** To make a print, pull a full sheet of paper from the packet under safelight. Lift up the easel masks and slide the paper against the stops. Gently lower the easel masks onto the paper, making sure that it does not move.

**2** Put your hand under the lens to block off the light and turn on the enlarger. Wait for ten seconds or so for the vibrations to die down. Swing your hand clear to start the exposure. Start timing at once.

### Improve blacks

Many amateur prints lack punch because the blacks are weak. To ensure full blacks:

● **Use glossy paper**, unless the print is to be displayed under highly directional lighting.

● **Always match** the developer and paper.

● **Always develop fully.** If you cut short the development time, some exposed grains may not be converted to black silver.

● **Never underexpose**, even if you overdevelop to increase contrast.

To make the most of the paper's capacity it must be fully exposed.

● **Test the maximum black** that a paper can give by fogging a sheet completely and developing for twice the recommended time.

● **Beware of vibration** during the exposure. It can blur a print just as badly as camera shake can blur a negative. Do not move around the room.

● **Use an exposure timer**, if you have one, to start and end the exposure; it will minimize vibration.

● **Do not touch the enlarger** during the exposure. Take particular care when dodging or burning in.

● **Print at night** when traffic is light if vibrations from passing lorries or trains are a problem.

● **Do not walk about** during the exposure – loose floorboards may shake the enlarger.

● **If light spills** from the lamphouse of your enlarger, it may fog the print. Paint the wall behind matt black to cut down any reflection.

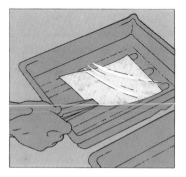

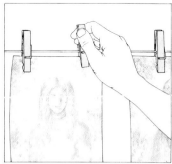

**3** At the end of the tested exposure time, switch off the enlarger. Draw the paper from the easel and transfer to the developer. Develop the print for the recommended time.

**4** After rinsing in a stop bath, fix the print for three minutes. Then transfer to fresh fixer and fix for a further three minutes, agitating continuously. Wash and dry the print normally.

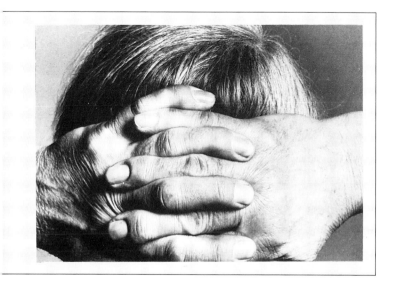

# Burn in Highlights

With some negatives, contrast is so extreme that you cannot get good detail in the highlights, even on the softest grade of paper, without badly overexposing the shadows. Printing on soft paper may rob the picture of all its impact anyway, as mid tones and shadows merge indistinguishably. The solution is to use the grade of paper that is correct for all but the highlights and then 'burn in' the highlights. This is done simply by giving the whole print the correct exposure, then masking all but the highlights while a further exposure is made.

● **Burn in the sky** in landscape pictures. The contrast between sky and land is often so great that all the sky is pale and uninteresting in a straight print. By burning in the sky, you can restore cloud detail and give the sky a little tone and drama. Be careful not to overdo it.

● **Use your hands for masking** as much as possible. Using hands gives a you a much better 'feel' for the technique and encourages you to make subtle improvements which you might ignore if working with cut-out masks.

● **Use a foot-switch** to control the enlarger in order to leave your hands free for print exposure control.

● **Stop down the lens** to give a long enough exposure for you to burn in in a controlled way.

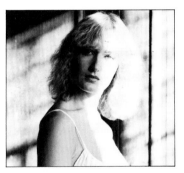

◀ In a straight print, the highlights, such as girl's hair, are almost pure white. To flesh out the highlights, I cut out a card mask for the entire print, leaving a hole for the highlight areas. First I exposed the whole print for 20 seconds. Then I held the mask over the paper to burn in the highlights for a further 12 seconds to give the print above. While burning in, I moved the mask continuously to prevent a hard edge line appearing in the print.

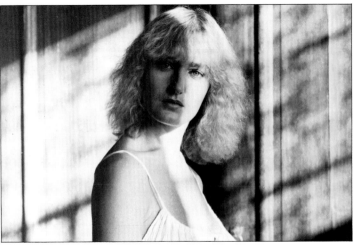

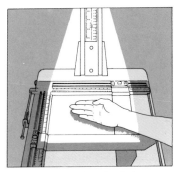

▲ You can shade the print during exposure to burn in highlights by moving your hand continuously over all the print except the highlights.

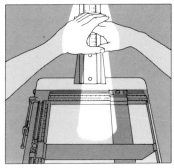

▲ Keep your hands closer to the lens for a soft burn in, and closer to the baseboard for clearly defined local exposure control.

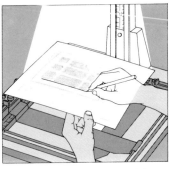

▲ For burning in elaborate highlight shapes, it is worth making a card mask. To make the mask, place a piece of card under the enlarger and mark out the highlight areas. Cut these from the card with a scalpel.

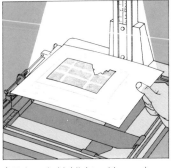

▲ To burn in highlights with a card mask, make the normal print exposure. Switch off the enlarger and move the card into place. Switch on the enlarger again. Keep the mask moving to prevent it showing on the print as a hard edge.

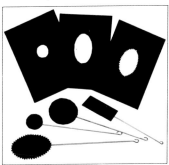

▲ You can make a variety of all-purpose masks for both burning in and dodging (see page 60). Dodging masks should be held on the end of a thin rigid wire.

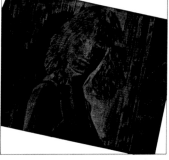

▲ To exert fine control over tones in the picture, make masks of tissue paper. By varying the number of layers of tissue, you can control the exposure precisely.

# Dodge Shadows

Just as some prints are improved by burning in the highlights, you can 'dodge' shadows to ensure that detail and tone are retained. Dodging, like burning in, uses masks to control the exposure received by different areas of the print. The difference is that dodging entails holding back the exposure in the shadows while exposing the rest of the print normally.

● **Establish local exposure** with the aid of test strips.

● **Pivot the wire handle** around the image when dodging near the centre of the print – otherwise the white shadow of the wire may appear in the print.

● **Keep the masks moving** while dodging and burning in to soften the edges of the masked area so that it merges with the print.

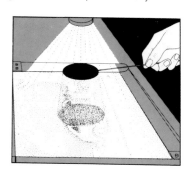

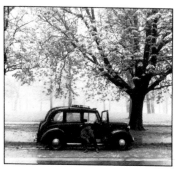

◀ In a straight print from this negative, the London taxi driver is lost in the shadow of his cab. To stop the cab and driver going so dark, I decided to dodge the print. The exposure for the straight print was 20 seconds, so I exposed the whole print for ten seconds and then held a simple circular dodging mask over the cab for the remaining 10 seconds exposure. The result was that the cab driver was rendered lighter and became clearly visible against the dark of the cab.

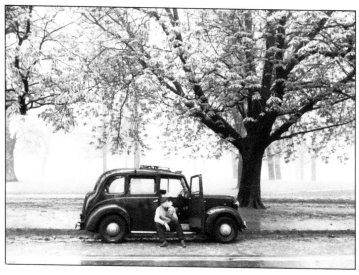

# Control Local Contrast

With VC paper, you can control contrast. If the contrast in one area of the print needs boosting or cutting back, you can use masks in the same way as burning in and dodging exposure. The contrast rating of VC paper varies according to the colour of the filter it is printed through. This means that by printing some areas of the print through one colour filter and others through another colour, you can achieve the contrast you want in each part of the picture. Bear in mind that the exposure needed may vary with the contrast grade used. Remember that Grades 4–5 need twice the exposure of Grades 00–3½ when you calculate the exposure needed for each part of the picture.

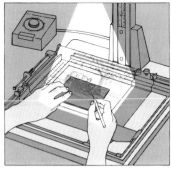

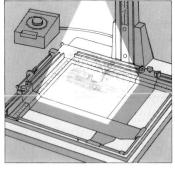

**1** To make local adjustments to contrast with VC paper, cut a mask from card to match the desired area. If you wish to boost tone separation in a shadow area, say, while retaining normal contrast elsewhere, cut a mask for the shadow area.

**2** After conducting a series of tests to establish the relative exposure that is needed, expose the entire print through the filter grade that is right for the area to be masked. For increased shadow contrast, expose through the hardest filter (Grade 5).

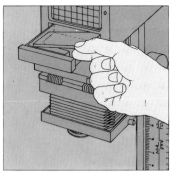

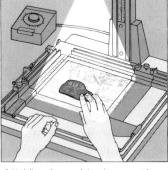

**3** After the correct exposure time for the area to be masked, switch off the enlarger. Carefully insert the filter that gives the right contrast for the remainder of the print. If the shadows are to be masked, use a softer filter (Grades 00 or 0).

**4** Holding the mask in place over the print, make the second part of the exposure. Usually, this part will be shorter since its purpose is mainly to fill in details and tone. Keep the edge of the mask moving during exposure to prevent it registering on the print.

# Vignette the Image

To give your pictures an old-fashioned look or to focus attention on the centre of the image, 'vignette' the print. In a vignetted print, the subject fades gradually into a black or white surround. A vignette is achieved, like burning in and dodging, by masking the required print area, but feathering the edges during exposure. A normal vignette brings the subject forward; a reversed vignette (with a black surround) creates an impression of depth.

▼ Prints vignetted against a dark surround tend to be moody and dramatic, and the effect is enhanced by similarly low-key lighting. The dark vignette below was made by first exposing normally for the whole print. Then the negative was removed from the enlarger and an oval mask was held just beneath the lens to mask the boy. The rest of the print was then thoroughly fogged by switching on the enlarger for three minutes with the aperture at the widest setting available.

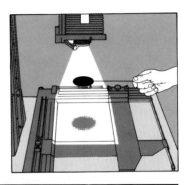

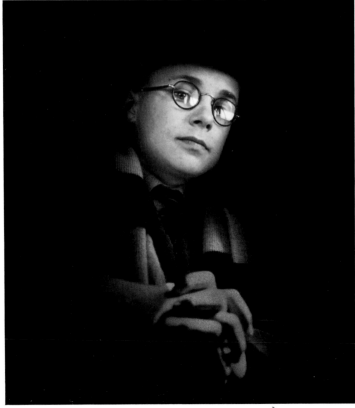

▼ Prints vignetted against a light surround are lighter in feel and work better if the lighting in the shot is pale and high-key. This is especially true if you want a period feel – perhaps because we expect old prints to have faded. To create a white vignette, cut out a mask with an oval hole in the centre. Then, holding this mask roughly half-way between the lens and the easel, make a normal exposure for the centre of the image. The picture below was then underdeveloped.

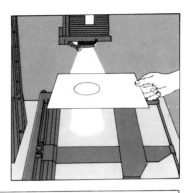

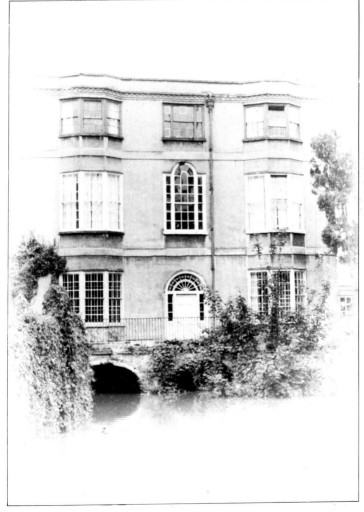

# Control Perspective

If you point your camera upwards to include the top of a tall building in the frame, you will inevitably find that all the vertical lines in the picture seem to converge unnaturally. This is in fact true perspective, but in a picture it looks very odd. Fortunately, you can align all but the most sharply converging verticals during printing by deliberately tilting the printing easel to distort the print, and then cropping to restore the shape.

● **Compose and focus** the image on the enlarger easel as usual.

● **Tilt the easel upwards** at the bottom end of the picture, so that it is nearer the lens. Note how the perspective straightens out.

● **Prop the easel** in place when the perspective seems natural.

● **Crop in,** as the part of the scene nearest the lens may be narrower than the masking frame on the baseboard.

● **Stop down the lens** to its smallest aperture to maximize depth of focus and keep all the print sharp.

● **Shade the print** progressively from top to bottom during exposure because the bottom is farther from the lens and needs more exposure.

▼ To frame the dome neatly in the archway while leaving a clean area of sky between, I had to get very close to the foreground: this meant that converging verticals were inevitable.

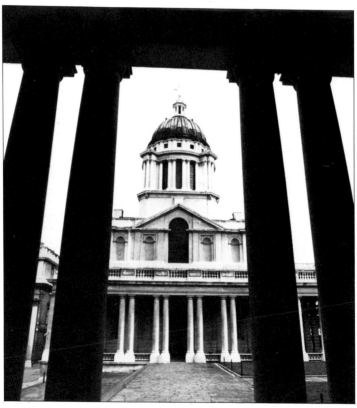

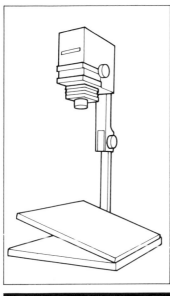

◀ The simplest way to correct converging verticals is to tilt the print paper by raising one side of the easel as shown. A similar effect can be achieved by tilting the enlarger head.

Unfortunately, the scope for correction by this method is limited by depth of focus. On some enlargers you can increase the depth of field when the easel is tilted by tilting the negative, lens and baseboard independently. By tilting the negative in the enlarger head one way, keeping the lens horizontal and tilting the easel the other, you can ensure all the image is in focus at quite steep angles.

▼ During printing I corrected the perspective to achieve this much more natural result by tilting the bottom of the picture up towards the enlarger lens to 'shrink' this end of the picture.

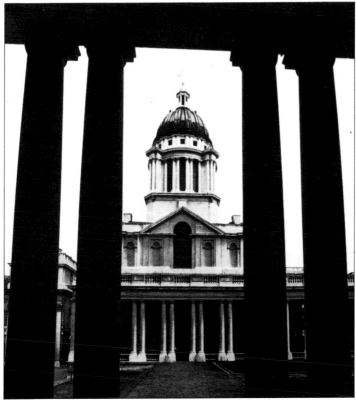

# Prepare for Colour

Colour processes have many similarities to black-and-white processes, and the equipment needed is substantially the same. However, all colour processes need a far greater degree of precision in time and temperature control – essentially because there are three emulsions, not one, and inaccuracies in processing throw out the colour balance. Precision is the key to success.

● **Use plastic tanks** for colour processing if you can. Stainless steel tanks may be affected by certain colour chemicals (notably bleach-fix solutions), and also take longer to empty, which can throw out timing of processes.

● **Measure temperature** with a mercury thermometer; spirit thermometers are not accurate enough for colour work. Alternatively, calibrate a spirit thermometer against a mercury thermometer (see page 17).

● **If you do a lot of colour work,** think about investing in a motorized rotary processor to help ensure accurate temperature control and agitation.

● **Use different containers** for your colour and black-and-white work if you can. Colour chemicals are very strong and may contaminate the black-and-white solutions unless the containers are cleaned with extreme care.

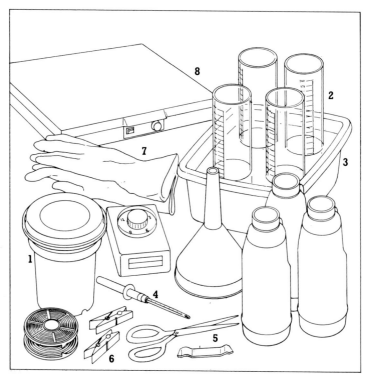

**What you need:**
1. Film processing tank
2. Graduates
3. Water bath for solutions
4. Precision thermometer
5. Scissors
6. Film clips
7. Rubber gloves
8. Tray warmer

## Colour negative process

| Kodak C-41 process | Processing stages | Temperature | Time (mins) |
|---|---|---|---|
| | Colour developer | 37.8±0.15°C | 3¼ |
| | Bleach | 24–40°C | 6½ |
| | Wash | 24–40°C | 3½ |
| | Fixer | 24–40°C | 6½ |
| | Wash | 24–40°C | 3½ |
| | Stabilizer | 24–40°C | 1½ |
| | Dry | | 10–20 |

Virtually all colour negative films can now be processed in Kodak's C-41 chemicals, or in compatible chemistry from other manufacturers. Kodak, Fuji, Konica, and Agfa films are all processed C-41, as are films from 'own-label' manufacturers such as department stores. The processing sequence above is for Kodak's own Hobby Pac, but most makers of darkroom chemicals market a C-41 kit. Some of these independent kits are very cheap and easy to use, combining bleach and fix to cut down process times and stages. Remember that you should take care when handling colour chemicals – some are very harmful. Wear rubber gloves, and ensure that all the bottles are properly labelled, and kept well out of the reach of children.

## Colour reversal (slide film) process

| E-6 process | Processing stages | Temperature | Time* (mins) |
|---|---|---|---|
| Kodak Ektachrome | | | |
| | First developer | 38±0.3°C | 6 |
| | Wash | 33–39°C | 1½–3 |
| | Reversal bath | 33–39°C | 1½–3 |
| | Colour developer | 38±0.6°C | 6–8 |
| | Conditioner | 30–40°C | 2 |
| | Bleach | 33–39°C | 6 |
| | Fix | 33–39°C | 3–6 |
| | Wash | 33–39°C | 1½–4 |
| | Stabilizer | 33–39°C | ½–3 |
| | Dry | below 60°C | |

*Times are given for a manual processor and will vary if a rotary processor is used.

All colour slide films can be processed at home, except Kodachrome. All other films are processed in Kodak's E-6 chemistry, or in comparable solutions from other manufacturers. The E-6 process was originally conceived for laboratories with automated processing machines, so solution temperatures are high, and process times short. Though it is not difficult to duplicate the process in the home darkroom, you need to take special care, and measure temperature and time with great accuracy, or colour casts will appear on your films. The process has two extra steps – first developer and reversal.

# Process Colour Negatives

The processing sequence for colour negatives varies according to the kit that you use, and it is important to follow the instructions to the letter. But with all processes, you need to pay meticulous attention to process times, temperatures and methodical agitation, especially during development. Unlike in black-and-white work, you cannot afford to ignore a 0.5°C (1°F) drop in temperature, or even the time it takes to fill and empty the tank. If you do not have a tempering bath to control temperature – and it is well worth getting one – make sure that the average temperature is correct. In other words, if the developer cools down by 2°C (3.5°F) during processing, start with the temperature 1°C (2°F) above the recommended temperature.

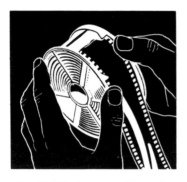

**1** Load the film into the tank in total darkness in exactly the same way as for ordinary black-and-white film. Because colour film is even more sensitive to fogging than black-and-white film, check once again that your loading area is absolutely light-proof.

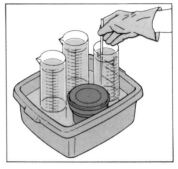

**2** Mix the chemicals carefully according to the maker's instructions, taking care not to cross-contaminate the solutions. Number the containers in the order in which they are to be used and bring them and the developing tank to the right temperature in the water bath.

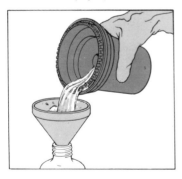

**5** Drain the tank after the allotted time, pouring reusable developer back into the bottle. Then refill the developing tank with bleach at the correct temperature. Remember that development continues until the tank is full of bleach, so solution changes must be timed precisely.

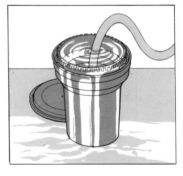

**6** Bleach for the set time, then drain and wash in running water. Take the lid off the tank to make washing easier if you wish. Remember to keep the water warm enough. After washing, check the fixer temperature, pour the fixer into the tank and start timing.

● **Start draining** the developer a little before the time is up to allow for the time it takes to drain the tank.

● **Take care** not to splash chemicals. Rinse away splashes immediately to avoid damage and stains.

● **Adjust washing time** according to the water temperature, within the range 24°–40°C (75–104°F).

● **Use water from the water bath** for the first few rinses of each wash then gradually add cooler water. Be sure the water bath is not contaminated, though.

● **Never** let the temperature of the water drop below 20°C (68°F).

● **Do not worry** about the milky appearance of the emulsion when it is wet. This disappears as the film dries.

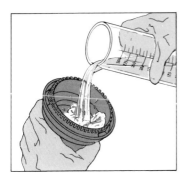

**3** Check the temperature of the developer and adjust if necessary. Pour the developer into the tank quickly but smoothly and start timing immediately. Tap the tank sharply on the bench to dislodge air bubbles trapped on the film. Begin to agitate at once.

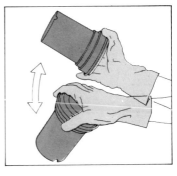

**4** Agitate according to the maker's instructions, and then check the temperature of the developer in the tank. If this has dropped, work out how much you will need to extend the development time to compensate. Stand the tank in the water bath between agitations.

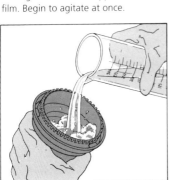

**7** At the end of the allotted fixing period, drain the tank once more and wash in running water. Where specified, pour in the stabilizer, and then dry without rinsing. Otherwise, give the film a final rinse in water treated with wetting agent.

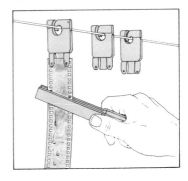

**8** Attach clips to the film and draw it from the spiral. Wipe it dry very carefully with a squeegee and hang it in a warm dust-free environment. Make sure that the temperature in the drying area does not rise above 45°C (113°F), or the emulsion may be damaged.

# Process Colour Slides

Colour slide film processing demands even greater precision perhaps than colour negative processing. This is because the slide is the finished product, and there is no opportunity to correct any minor faults during printing. Colour slide film processing is also a little more complex, for it has two extra steps. Instead of going straight into the colour developer which forms coloured dyes in exposed parts of the image, colour slide film is first developed to give a black-and-white negative image. This must then be 'reversed' to a positive before it can be colour developed – hence the name 'reversal' film. In E-6 processing, this reversal is achieved chemically: earlier transparency processes reversed the image by exposure to white light.

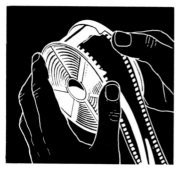

**1** Load the film into the tank in total darkness in exactly the same way as for colour negative and black-and-white film. Once the film is safely in the tank, stand the tank in the water bath in order to warm it up to the correct processing temperature.

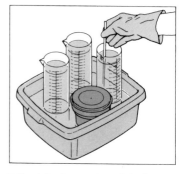

**2** Check the temperature of the first developer solution and adjust if necessary. With the tank on the bench, pour in the developer and start timing. Tap the tank sharply on the bench to dislodge air bubbles, and begin to agitate the tank.

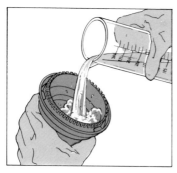

**5** Check the reversal bath temperature – it should be within 2°C (3.5°F) of the recommended temperature. Pour the reversal bath solution into the tank, and agitate by inversion as recommended. This bath usually lasts about two minutes.

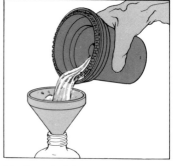

**6** At the end of the reversal step, pour the solution back into the bottle. All the process chemicals can be reused, but shelf-life varies: once mixed, the first developer, reversal bath and conditioner last only four weeks, but other solutions keep for 8–24 weeks.

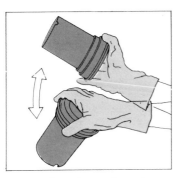

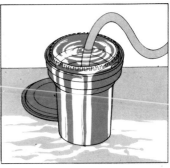

**3** Agitate the tank according to the process instructions, replacing the tank in the water bath between agitation periods to stop the solutions cooling. Monitor the temperature carefully during development, since errors will affect slide density.

**4** At the end of the first development time, drain the tank swiftly, and fill with wash water. You can use running water, or water from the water bath. The wash water temperature is less critical than that of the solutions, but should be within 3° of 36°C (5.5° of 96.8°F).

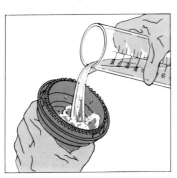

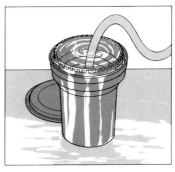

**7** Check the temperature of the colour developer and adjust it if necessary. Pour in the developer and start timing. Tap the tank to dislodge air bubbles, and agitate as indicated by the process manufacturers. Start draining the tank a little before time is up.

**8** Pour in the stop, wash or conditioner as directed, drain and pour in the bleach bath. After bleaching, wash if necessary, then add the fixer. Wash in running water for the recommended time, rinse in stabilizer if directed, and dry normally.

# Prepare to Print in Colour

Colour printing is the most demanding basic darkroom technique, calling for precise processing and fine control of the colour of the enlarger light by using coloured filters. Nevertheless, if you can handle black-and-white printing, there is no reason why you should not try colour. Modern processes and paper have removed much of the scope for error in colour printing, and you will find that the extra control over colour possible at home gives you prints that are much better than commercial machine prints.

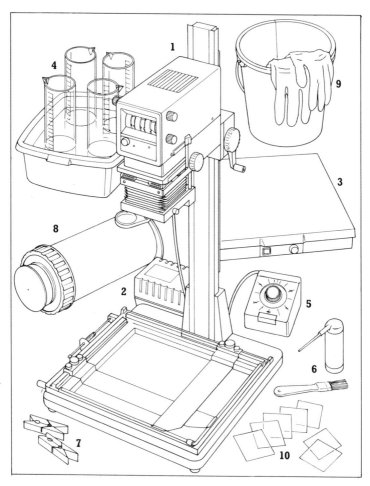

**What you need**

1. Enlarger with facilities for colour filtration
2. Voltage regulator
3. Tray warmer
4. Bowl, graduates and precision thermometer (see page 66)
5. Timer
6. Brush and compressed air for cleaning negatives
7. Pegs
8. Print processing tube
9. Rubber gloves
10. Set of acetate filters if your enlarger has no colour head

## Prints from negatives

| Kodak RA-4 | Processing stages | Temperature | Time (mins) |
|---|---|---|---|
| | Presoak | 38°C | ½ |
| | Developer | 38°C | 35 sec. |
| | Stop bath | 30–34°C | ¾ |
| | Bleach-fix | 30–34°C | ¾ |
| | Wash | 30–34°C | 2 |
| | Dry | below 99°C | |

## Reversal prints from slides

| Kodak Ektachrome R-3000 | Processing stages | Temperature | Time (mins) |
|---|---|---|---|
| | Presoak | 30°C | 1 |
| | First developer | 30°C | 2¾ |
| | Wash | 30°C | ⅓ |
| | Wash | 30°C | ⅓ |
| | Wash | 30°C | ⅓ |
| | Colour developer | 30°C | 5¼ |
| | Wash | 30±2°C | ⅓ |
| | Wash | 30±2°C | ⅓ |
| | Bleach-fix | 30°C | 4 |
| | Wash (running water) | 30±2°C | 2¼ |
| | Dry | below 99°C | |

## Ilfochrome prints from slides

| Processing stages | at 20°C (mins) | at 24°C (mins) | at 29°C (mins) |
|---|---|---|---|
| Pre-soak | – | – | ½ |
| Developer | 4 | 3 | 2 |
| Rinse | ½ | ½ | ½ |
| Bleach | 4 | 3 | 2 |
| Fix | 4 | 3 | 2 |
| Wash | 4 | 3 | 2 |

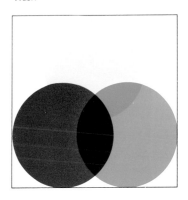

### Colour filters
Filters for colour printing by the subtractive method come in yellow, magenta and cyan. A full strength filter in each colour would subtract a third of the spectrum. The filters normally used, however, are much weaker than this.

# Test for Exposure

In printing from colour negatives, there are two variables to test for before you make each print: exposure and colour balance. You should always test for exposure first because without correct exposure you cannot get good colour balance. Testing for exposure with colour prints is similar to making tests for black-and-white prints, and the most reliable method is to make a test strip covering a range of exposure times. However, before you make the test, you must make sure that the enlarger light is roughly the right colour by selecting the basic filter pack or dial-in filter setting given with the printing paper. This varies widely according to the film/paper combination from zero filtration to settings such as 50 magenta 90 yellow 0 cyan.

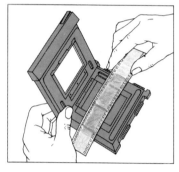

**1** Dust your chosen negative and place it in the negative carrier with the emulsion (dull side) down. Switch on the enlarger and switch off the room lights. With the enlarger lens at full aperture, compose and focus the image on the easel in the normal way.

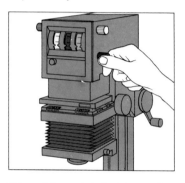

**2** Consult the packet of print paper for the recommended starting filtration. If your enlarger has a dial-in colour head, adjust the controls accordingly. If not, make up a filter pack, using as few filters as possible, and insert the pack in the filter drawer.

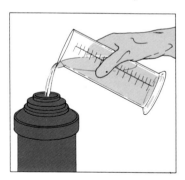

**5** Prepare all the solutions and bring them to the correct temperature in a water bath. Fill the print drum with water at the pre-soak temperature. Leave for one minute, agitating occasionally to ensure all the print is warm, then drain the drum.

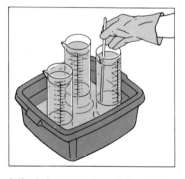

**6** Check the temperature of the solutions and adjust if necessary. Pour the developer into the drum. Some drums are filled upright, and processing begins when you lay them down. Others are loaded lying down and processing starts when you roll them.

● **Use a UV filter** as well as the colour balance filters.

● **Use a full sheet** of paper for the test unless your processing drum will take smaller sheets.

● **Identify the emulsion** side of the paper by its sticky feel.

● **Clean and dry the drum** thoroughly to remove dust before loading the exposed film.

● **Process the same way** every time to ensure predictable results.

● **Keep the drum** level during processing to prevent the solutions draining to one end.

● **Speed dry test prints** with a hair dryer, keeping the print cooler than 93°C (200°F).

● **With a rotary drum,** process under safelight until after fixing.

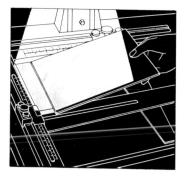

**3** Stop down the lens to *f*11 and switch off the enlarger. In total darkness or under a Wratten 13 safelight, place a sheet of print paper on the easel. Make a test strip in the same way as for black-and-white prints, but move the card every five seconds up to a total of 25.

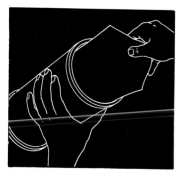

**4** Gently curve the exposed paper and load it into the processing drum with the emulsion facing inwards. Seal the lid of the drum tightly and check that there is no unexposed paper lying uncovered. Switch on the lights and prepare to process.

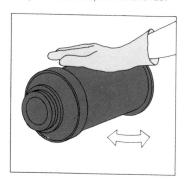

**7** Lay down or roll the drum to start development. Start timing at once. Agitate by rolling the drum back and forth on the bench once every two seconds, or as instructed. Drain the drum, starting ten seconds before the end of the allotted time.

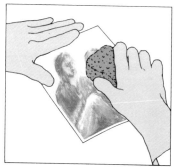

**8** Repeat steps 6 and 7 for the stop and bleach-fix baths, then remove the print from the drum, handling it carefully by the edges. Wash it under warm running water for the recommended time to remove all the chemicals. Dry the print with a hair dryer.

# Test for Colour

When you are examining the test print for the right exposure time, you may notice that the colours are not quite right. Only rarely does the starting filtration give perfect colour balance. Usually, the first test print has a slight colour cast, and the next step is to neutralize this. This means making another test print, with a range of filter combinations rather than exposure times. To select the range of filtration, you must roughly identify the cast. If the colours in the first test print look warm, the cast is yellow, red or magenta. If they look cold, suspect a green, cyan or blue cast. For the colour test, add a little filtration of the cast's colour to the starting filtration, and try a range of close combinations. Make sure that you only compare dry prints with dry to establish colour casts.

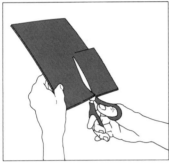

**1** For the colour test, divide the print into quadrants rather than narrow bands to ensure that each area is representative of the whole print. Start by cutting a quarter away from a piece of opaque card large enough to cover the entire print area.

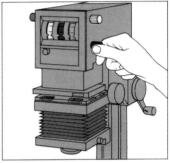

**2** Write down the four different filter settings to be used in the test. Dial in the first new setting on the colour head or make up a filter pack, using as few filters as possible – use one 20M filter rather than two 10Ms. Switch off the room lights.

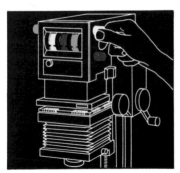

**5** Take the print paper from the easel and store it somewhere light-proof. Switch on the room lights and dial in the filtration needed for the second part of the test or make up an appropriate filter pack. Work out the change in exposure needed.

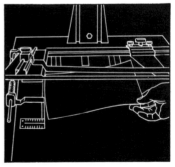

**6** Switch off the room light and retrieve the partially exposed paper from its temporary storage. Replace the paper in the easel, using the snipped-off corner to guide you. The paper must be in exactly the same position as it was for the first exposure.

● **Do not overdo filtration.** A 10 unit change corrects most pale colour casts.

● **To correct** a warm cast, try adding 10Y, 10Y + 10M, and 10M to the filtration. To correct a cold cast, try subtracting 10Y, 10Y + 10M and 10M.

● **Never combine** all three colours of filter in one print. Instead, subtract the values of the weakest colour from the values of the others.

● **Adjust the exposure** according to the recommended filter factors for each change in filtration.

● **Identify a cast** more precisely by looking at the first test print briefly through a range of filters. Once you find a filter combination that gives good colour, note the values and then use half these values in the filter pack.

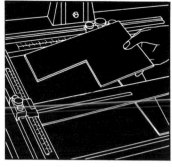

**3** Take out a fresh sheet of paper and snip off one corner. This will help you to position the print the right way round for each part of the test. Place the paper in the easel and lay the opaque card in place so that all but one quadrant is masked.

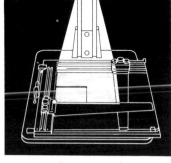

**4** Expose the first quadrant for the time determined by the exposure test, adjusted to take into account the new filtration. When the exposure is over, switch off the enlarger and lift the card. Lay it on the bench in exactly the same orientation.

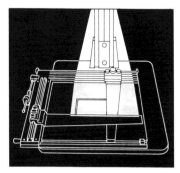

**7** Flip the card mask over to uncover a new quadrant. Lay the card in position over the easel and make the second exposure in exactly the same way. Repeat the procedure for the other two test quadrants, adjusting the filtration and exposure for each quadrant.

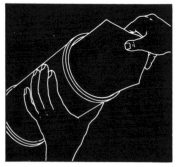

**8** Process the colour test print in the same way as the exposure test. When the print is dry, examine it in good, bright light. If no quadrant gives correct colour, make a third test. Otherwise, you can make a full print, using the values established by the tests.

# Balance Colour

Quadrant tests enable you to get fairly close to the filtration needed for correct colour, but it can often be very difficult to fine tune the colour. The problem lies in identifying the colour of the remaining cast. Cast identification becomes easier with experience, but to begin with, it is worth making a colour 'ring-around' chart as a reference. The numbers below each print indicate the density of the filters needed to correct the cast.

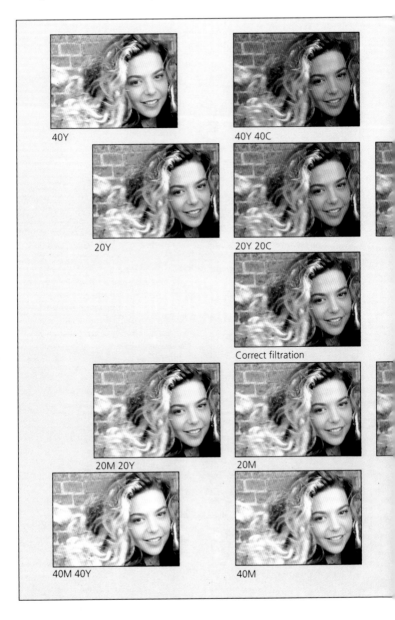

40Y

40Y 40C

20Y

20Y 20C

Correct filtration

20M 20Y

20M

40M 40Y

40M

● **Look for a second colour**. Not all casts have a single component. A print with a magenta cast may also have a red tinge, making the print orangey.

● **Find a secondary cast** by making a test print to correct the predominant cast, then identify the filtration needed to correct the remaining cast.

● **Remember** that to correct a red cast you need yellow and magenta filtration, for a blue cast magenta and cyan, and for a green cast cyan and yellow.

◀ A colour ring-around provides an invaluable reference chart with which you can compare your test prints to help you to identify any cast that may be present. The chart is essentially a series of prints made from a good, typical negative, each with a different, carefully controlled colour cast.

To make a ring-around, select a well-exposed negative with a good range of tones and colours, preferably including flesh tones, since these are particularly sensitive to colour imbalances. From this negative, make a correctly exposed, correctly colour-balanced print and note down the filtration.

Starting with this filtration as a base, make a series of small prints, progressively changing the filter pack by 20 units for each of the six possible combinations of filters: yellow, yellow and magenta, magenta, magenta and cyan, cyan, cyan and yellow. Arrange these prints on white card in the manner shown and write down the filtration needed to correct the cast alongside. The filtration needed is simply the filtration you gave to create the cast removed. So where you gave 40Y 40M, for instance, the cast is corrected by subtracting 40Y 40M from the filter pack (or alternatively, adding 40C). The filters used here are Kodak.

To find the filtration needed to correct future prints, simply compare the test print with your ring-around chart. When you find an image in the ring-around with a cast that matches the test print in colour, read off the filtration and adjust the filtration for the main print accordingly.

If your pictures are rarely portraits, you can do a ring-around for a subject that you often shoot (eg, a landscape).

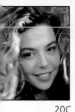

40C

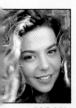

20C

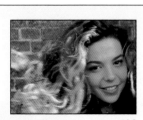

20C 20M

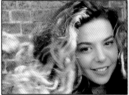

40C 40M

# Print from Slides

To make prints from slides, photographers often used to copy the slide onto negative film to make an 'internegative'. This negative would then be printed in the normal way. Nowadays, however, it is just as easy to print the slide directly onto 'pos/pos' paper, so called because it gives a positive print from a positive original. Pos/pos paper is of two main types, reversal papers and Ilfochrome. Reversal papers work in the same way as most other colour processes, forming dyes during processing. Like colour slides, the image is made positive by reversal processing. In contrast, in the Ilfochrome process, dyes are present in the unexposed print and are destroyed selectively. The processing sequence below is for reversal papers.

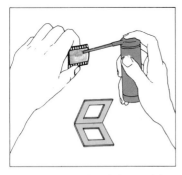

**1** To make a print directly from a slide, remove the slide from its mount and clean it using a soft brush or a compressed air jet. Insert the slide into the negative carrier and place it in the enlarger. Focus and compose the image in the usual way.

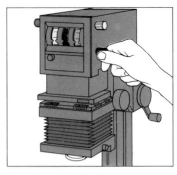

**2** Set the starting filtration according to the directions on the paper pack. Switch off the room lights and place a sheet of reversal paper on the easel in total darkness – there is no safelight for pos/pos papers. Place a piece of card ready for a test print.

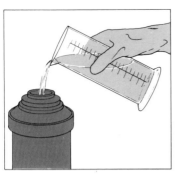

**5** Pour in the first developer, and start development. Agitate in the same way as for colour negative printing. Begin to drain the drum ten seconds before development is up. Give a stop bath if advised, then wash well in two minute-long baths of fresh warm water.

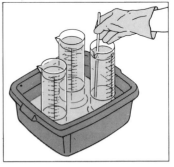

**6** Check the temperature of the colour developer, and adjust it if necessary. Pour the solution into the drum and start timing. Accuracy is vital, for it is during this stage that the silver negative image is reversed to a positive and the colour dye image forms.

● **If the print is too dark,** increase the exposure – opposite to prints made from negatives.

● **Identify the cast** by comparing the test with the slide.

● **Correct colour casts** when printing from slides by subtracting filters of the same colour or adding filters of the other two colours. Change filtration in units of 15 or more.

● **For Ilfochrome prints,** the procedure is similar, although Ilford recommend a quadrant for all tests. But Ilfochrome prints must be processed in their own chemicals in the following sequence: pre-soak; developer; rinse; bleach; fix and wash. For timings, see page 73.

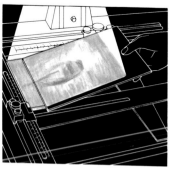

**3** Make a series of test exposures in the same way as for colour negative printing (see pages 74–5). For an 8 x 10in print with a starting filtration of 45C 45M, make the test exposures at intervals of 2,4, 8 and 16 seconds with the lens set at an aperture of *f*8.

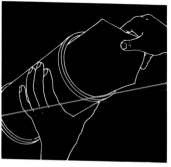

**4** After exposing the test print, load it into the processing drum and turn on the lights. Fill the tank with warm water at the same temperature as the first developer. During the pre-soak, check the temperature of the first developer, and adjust it if necessary.

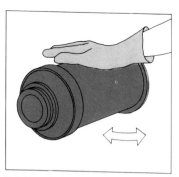

**7** Agitate during colour development by rolling the tank on the bench or, better still, using a motorized drum roller. After colour development, wash briefly and pour in the bleach-fix. Then wash again, use a stabilizing bath if specified, and wash again.

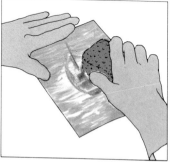

**8** Wipe away excess water and dry as you would prints from negatives. When dry, select the exposure band and make a quadrant test (see page 76–7), adjusting filtration and exposure as above. Repeat until you have a perfect quadrant, then make the final print.

# Combine Slide Images

One great advantage of using colour slide film is that the results are easy to manipulate. By sandwiching two slides together, you can see immediately what a combination image will look like. By comparison, combining images in the darkroom is much more time-consuming, and requires a greater degree of skill. Sandwiching is not the only technique that you can use; with a slide copier, such as the apparatus shown at the foot of the facing page, you can combine images additively – adding a setting sun, for example, to a lyrical landscape.

### Sandwiching slides
This is the easiest way to combine images on slide.

● **Pick thin images** – normal slides look too dark when sandwiched.

● **Choose one main image** and use the other to add texture, colour, or some other simple element. If both images are rich in detail, they will compete.

● **Clean the slides** then fix them together as shown opposite.

▼ This image was created simply by sandwiching together two slides – the hang-glider was on one, and the sunset on the other.

### Additive copying
By using a slide copier (opposite below), you can make two exposures, in order to record first one image, then a second, onto a single piece of film.

● **Pick one original** with a clear dark area – such as blue sky. Copy this in the normal way, then tension the camera's shutter without advancing the film.

● **The second slide** should have light detail only in the area that was dark on the first slide. By copying the second image, you will drop the light detail from the second image into the dark area of the first slide.

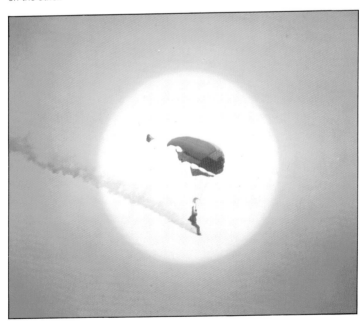

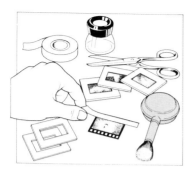

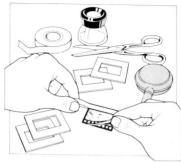

**1** Start sandwiching by carefully cleaning both slides, and laying a strip of double-sided tape along the edge of the first image. Make sure that a sliver of tape does not intrude into the image area.

**2** Before you remove the non-adherent backing from the tape, carefully align the second image and check for positioning. Then peel off the backing, and press the two slides together.

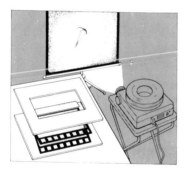

**3** Finally, mount the slide in the normal way, ready for projection. Take care to secure the slide mount, because the two pieces of film may push apart the sides of a mount designed for just a single layer. The best mounts to use are those designed for audio-visual presentations. These slide mounts have glass cover plates that press the two images together, so that they both remain in focus when projected.

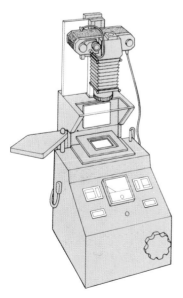

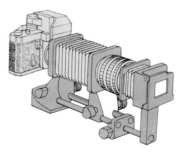

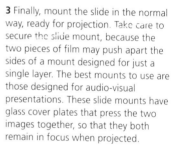

### Slide Copiers
To combine images additively, use a slide copier. The copier above fits onto the end of a bellows unit, and allows you to enlarge or reduce one or both elements. The unit on the left has extra features: you can control contrast, and exposure control is semi-automatic. Bracket both parts of a multiple exposure to get different effects.

# Make Photograms

You can make simple photographs called 'photograms' in the darkroom without even a camera. All you need is print paper, a light source – the enlarger is ideal – and a selection of objects to place in the light path. When the enlarger is switched on, the paper is exposed everywhere but in the shadow of the objects in the light path. So the paper records a negative image – a silhouette in reverse – of the object. Although the principle is simple, you can create some subtle and delicate effects by varying the position of the objects, the character of the light, and the paper.

● **Collect interesting shapes** for making photograms, or use everyday, fairly flat, objects such as keys or coins.

● **Use black-and-white paper** for opaque objects, or colour the light source strongly.

● **Use any photographic material** you choose for translucent objects.

● **Plan your image in daylight.**

● **Set the aperture** at *f*11 and make a test strip, starting at about ten seconds.

● **Process normally,** assess the test, and make a full photogram.

● **Try translucent objects** in the negative carrier.

● **Place small objects** in the negative carrier of your enlarger for the most exciting photograms.

● **For negative carrier photograms** place a glass plate or sheet of strong acetate in the carrier.

● **Focus the enlarger** with a small pin resting on the glass.

● **Suspend objects** that will not fit in the negative carrier in the lens housing, using fine cotton, clear tape or something else that will not show.

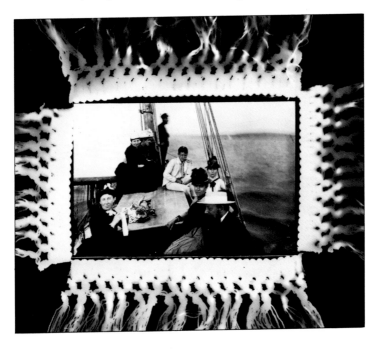

▼ This photogram was very easy to make and involved arranging cogs, punch tape, springs and various other objects on a piece of print paper under safelight, then exposing under the enlarger. However, to make a slightly more interesting photogram and give it a little depth, I printed on soft paper to retain mid-grey tones and shaded and dodged the photogram during exposure.

◄ Opposite, photogram techniques were used to create a border around a normal print.

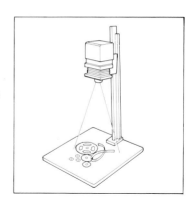

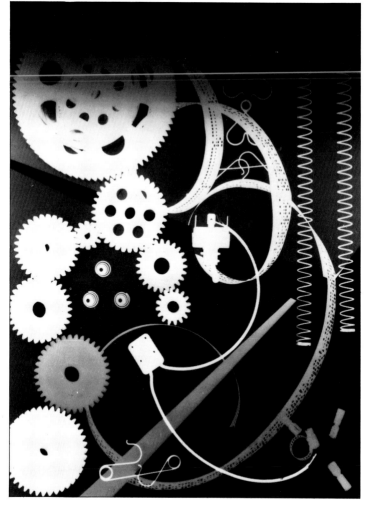

# Expose through Glass

One of the easiest ways of adding interest to a black-and-white print is to retexture it during the printing process. Almost any material capable of passing light will lend a characteristic pattern to the image: you can print through tracing paper, a piece of stocking, or even lace curtains. The pictures on these pages were made by printing through various types of glass.

● **To soften an image,** place a sheet of diffusing glass just above, or just below, your enlarger lens for part of the exposure.

● **Experiment with colour** printing paper and glass streaked with watercolour.

● **To produce a pattern,** place a sheet of textured glass in contact with either the negative or the paper. Place the textured side against the paper.

● **Smear petroleum jelly** on glass for a rippled effect.

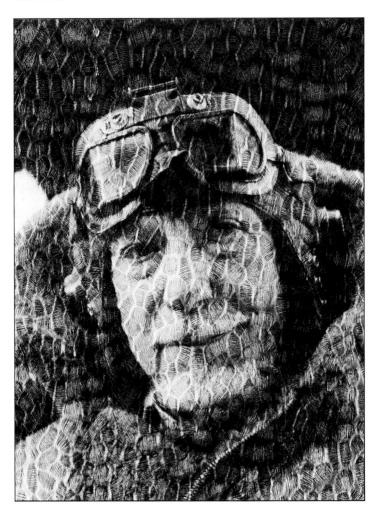

▶ The result of printing an image through the kind of rippled glass used to glaze bathroom windows was a pseudo-reticulation effect (opposite). A grained glass, similar to that used in diffusion screens, or as the focusing screens of view cameras, produced the image on the right; and a veined glass of the kind used to reduce strong directional light created the effect below. In each case, the sheet of glass was laid over the printing paper before the exposure was made. Although the overall impression was to be fairly soft, I decided to use a contrasty grade of paper, Grade 5. This helped to bring out the pattern of the glass very clearly and creates an effect reminiscent of a printer's half-tone screen.

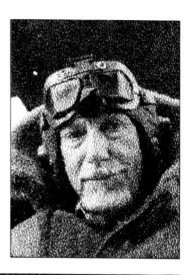

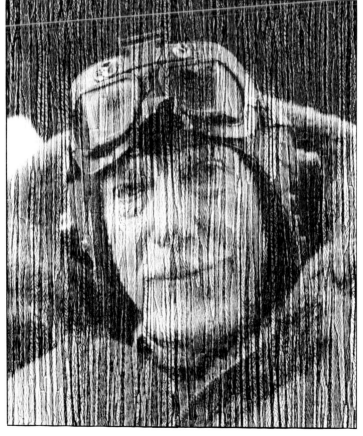

# Eliminate Tones

By using lith film, you can eliminate shades of grey from a black-and-white print and create stark, graphic images from almost any negative. Lith film (a special material borrowed from the printing industry) is easy to use, and anyone who can make high-quality black-and-white prints should have little trouble using this extremely high-contrast material.

● **Use a red safelight** when working with lith film. Lith film may be fogged by the amber safelight recommended for ordinary printing paper.

● **Buy lith film in sheets,** or in 35mm rolls. 35mm film is cheaper but much less easy to use than 5 x 4in sheet film.

● **Use a special developer** such as Tetenal Dokulith or vignette lith developer. This is packed in the form of dry crystals in two bags marked 'A' and 'B'. Make up two stock solutions by diluting each with water. Keep these separate until the moment you are ready to develop the film.

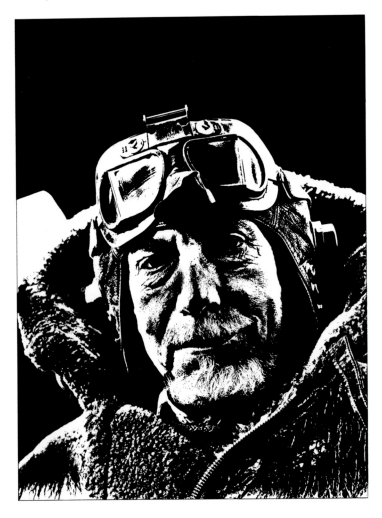

● **Make up the developer** according to the instructions.

● **Wear rubber gloves** when handling lith chemicals. They are very caustic and may cause dermatitis.

● **Use the developer promptly,** as it deteriorates very rapidly. Once it turns yellow, discard it.

● **To make a print,** expose the lith positive in contact with another sheet of lith to give a negative and use this to print with, or …

● **… Print the positive** to give an unusual negative image.

◀ To eliminate the tones from the original and create this rather striking effect, I printed the negative onto lith film under the enlarger, retouching the image with opaque dye where it was necessary. I made a negative by contact printing, and then a positive print from this negative.

● **Make a test strip** to find the exposure, but use only small steps (2, 4, 6, 8, 10, 12 seconds) for each band because lith film has very little exposure latitude.

● **Expose sheets of lith** under the enlarger like ordinary prints.

● **Develop sheets of lith** film in print processing trays for 2¾ minutes at 20°C (68°F). Handle the film with rubber gloves rather than tongs to avoid scratches.

● **Agitate continuously** for the first two minutes, then leave still for the rest of the development time.

▼ I made this high-contrast portrait of the poet Robert Graves from a black-and-white slide. To eliminate the tones, I simply exposed the slide in contact with a short strip of 35mm lith film in a contact proof printer. After processing, I printed the resulting lith negative in the normal way.

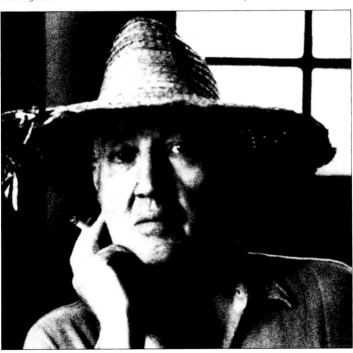

# Solarize in Black and White

One way of turning a fairly ordinary photograph into an attractive image is to solarize it. True solarization (a 1000-times overexposure) is difficult, but you can get much the same result using the Sabattier effect. This process, which involves exposing a print to light during development, is a little uncertain, so experiment to get what you want and do not expect to be able to repeat it exactly.

● **Select a simple image** and make a normal print on Grade 5 paper for reference. Too complicated an image will yield a confusing print.

● **Make a second print,** but instead of developing it, put it away in a light-proof envelope or in a paper safe.

● **Remove the negative** from the enlarger. Using just white light from the enlarger, make a test strip (see page 54). Develop this for half the time that was needed to develop the reference print fully and completely.

● **Note the exposure** that gives a middle grey tone. This is the fogging exposure for the Sabattier effect.

● **Cover the enlarger** baseboard with a towel and place a dish of water on it.

● **Take the exposed sheet** of paper from its envelope and develop it for half the normal time. Slide it into the water, disturbing the surface as little as possible.

● **Let the ripples die away.**

● **Fog the print** by switching on the enlarger for the time established by the test strip.

● **Complete development** by developing the print again for half the normal time.

● **Fix and wash** the completed print in the usual way.

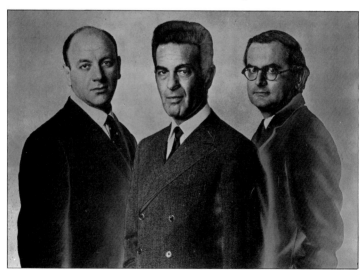

▲ Black-and-white film can be solarized in exactly the same way as can black-and-white prints, by contact printing onto lith film, developing for half of the time calculated, fogging with white light and completing development. A second way to solarize a black-and-white print is to print onto high-contrast paper and then re-expose the print to white light for a second or two half-way through development. Do not agitate during development.

▼ The solarized black-and-white print of the model needed some supporting background. I chose the staircase first, then the image of the trees, overexposed about 100 times, was montaged onto the steps. Finally, I added the image of the Mallard drake in order to introduce an element into the foreground that would lead the viewer's eye into the picture. Solarization of the entire image would have proved too confusing.

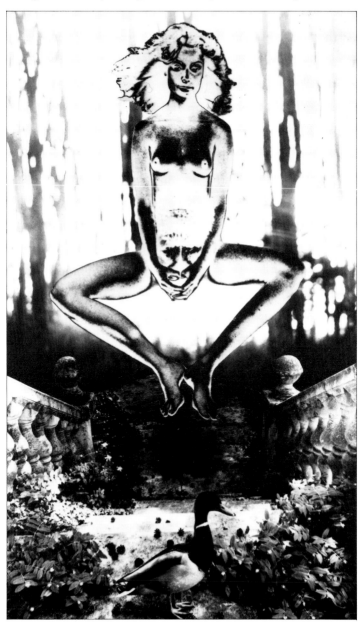

# Cross Processing

Processing colour film in the 'wrong' chemicals has become an increasingly popular technique for creating weird-looking pictures. The procedure involves developing a colour print film in colour transparency chemistry – or vice versa. How the colours in your picture change will depend on the make of film, the exposure and the length of development. Slight changes in these factors can make huge differences to your results, so experiment.

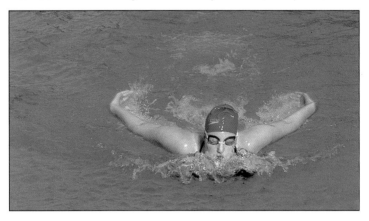

● **Cross processing** normally gives an overall colour shift towards cyan, green or magenta. Changing film type will allow you to find different effects.

● **The technique** always increases the contrast of the picture, so it is usually best to use low-contrast lighting to begin with. Grain will also be increased.

● **Effective film speed** will decrease, so allow for this when exposing or processing the film, or both.

● **Start by overexposing** colour print film by two or three stops, and then push process it by two stops when using E6 (transparency) chemistry. So, an ISO 400 colour print film should be exposed at ISO 100 or ISO 50 – and then development should be extended.

● **When using colour slide film,** increase exposure by about two stops, and then process the film through C-41 colour print chemistry normally.

● **Bracket widely** (from 3 stops under to 3 stops over, in 1-stop stages) to ensure that you have a range of effects.

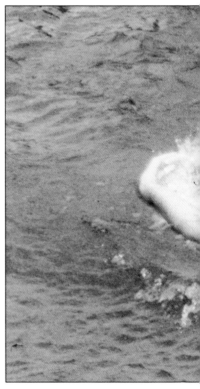

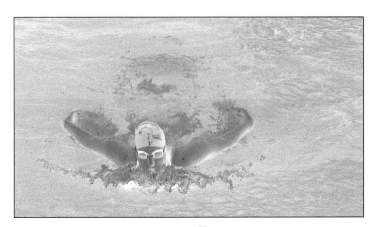

● **If you are not processing** the film yourself, use a professional laboratory that is used to dealing with cross-processing. Label your films with your exact processing requirements so that there are no misunderstandings that may ruin your work.

▼ The picture below was taken by overexposing colour transparency film and processing it in C-41 chemicals. The negative can be seen above. The final result is a high contrast, grainy picture that has markedly changed colour from the original, straight image (left).

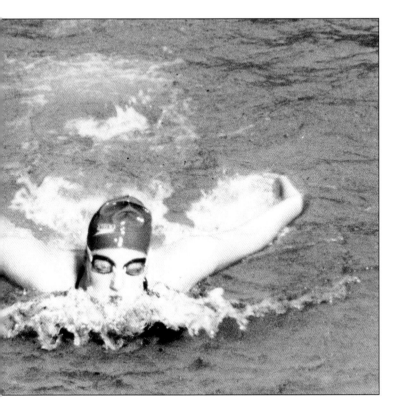

# Combine Prints

Combining two or more pictures is a way of creating an entirely new image. The simplest method is to sandwich two negatives together in the enlarger, but multiple printing – exposing two or more negatives one after the other onto the same piece of paper – means that you can print the second image at whatever size and in whatever position you want.

● **Plan the final image** on paper by projecting each negative in turn and tracing the outlines of the elements.

● **Use the tracing** as a hinged overlay so that you can size and focus each negative correctly.

● **Make a test print** for each negative.

● **Use two enlargers** if you can, moving the masking frame from one to the other.

● **Shade each image** during exposure with masks and dodgers cut to shapes that match elements in the final print.

● **Add reflections** to a picture by printing the top half of the negative while masking off the bottom half of the print and then turning the negative through 180° and masking off the already exposed area of the print.

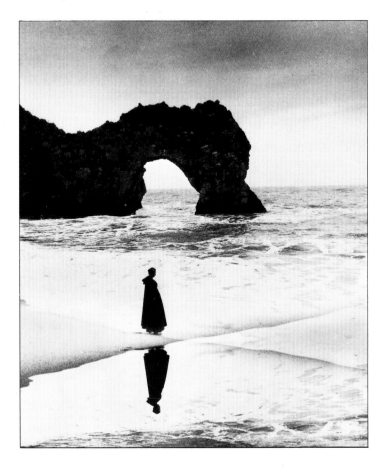

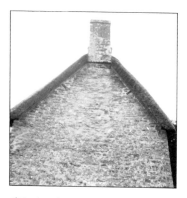

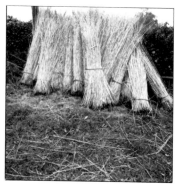

◀ The beach area was masked off and the image printed right way up. The negative was then turned through 180° and the masking frame moved to print in the girl and the sea.

▲ The outlines of the cottage and the sheaves were traced on card. The cut card was used to mask first the area for the sheaves and then the area in which the cottage had been printed.

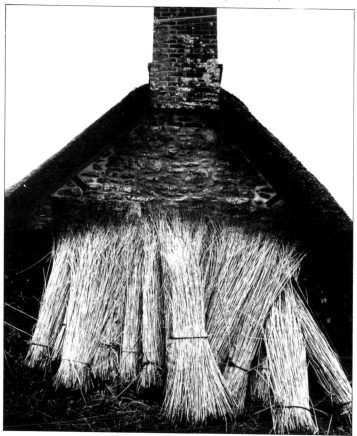

# Montage in Black and White

Few darkroom techniques provide more scope for creativity or just sheer fun than photomontage. By simply cutting out parts of some prints and sticking them down on another print, you can create virtually any image you want. Bizarre, amusing, realistic, poignant – whatever you choose. Prints can be montaged in many ways, but there are two main approaches. Montages can either be 'rough cut' so that all the joins show up clearly, and there is no doubt that the picture is a montage, or the joins can be hidden so that the picture seems to be just one photograph.

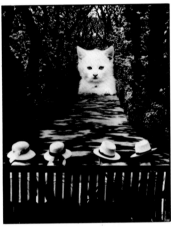

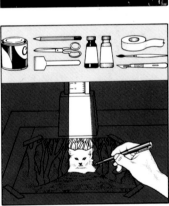

▼ I photographed this sequence with a montage in mind. Motor-drive shots can work well when montaged together.

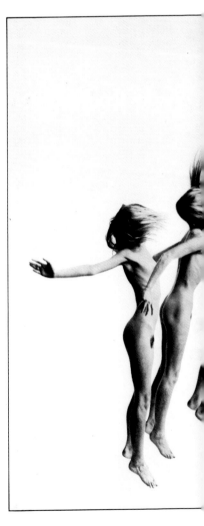

▲ This bizarre image was created by montaging two prints with invisible join techniques. After making a print of the park background, I traced in the cat's head and made a print on single weight matt paper to the right size. I then cut a rough outline, scored accurately around the cat's head and carefully tore away the excess before pasting in place.

● **Lay tracing paper** over a large print of your background and draw in the outlines of the new elements.

● **Transfer the tracing** onto the enlarger baseboard to make prints to the right size.

● **Match print characteristics** – paper grade, exposure and elements such as perspective – if you want invisible joins.

● **Cut a rough outline** leaving an inch to spare around the subject.

● **Run a scalpel along** the outline. Make a series of right-angle cuts from the outline to the score mark.

● **Gently tear** away the rough outline. Sandpaper away unwanted fibres and darken the edges with a soft pencil.

● **Stick the cut-out** down in place on the background print, pressing from the centre out.

● **Retouch any weak areas** that there may be, then photograph and reprint the finished montage.

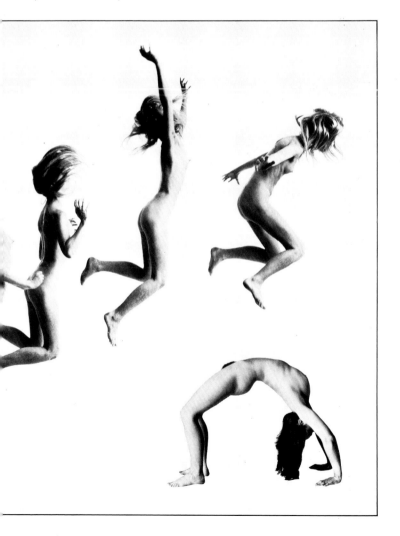

# Montage in Colour

Montage in black and white can produce fascinating results, but the additional dimension of colour gives you even more scope to create strange and intriguing images. Colour prints are far more expensive than black and white, though, and it is important to cut waste to a minimum by carefully planning each image in advance.

● **Colour print papers** are now all of the RC type, so extra care is needed when montaging, and it is important to use water-based dyes rather than oils when retouching to disguise joins.

● **Match colour** carefully even if trying to create a bizarre effect. Differences in colour bias will show up badly. Use the same batch of paper for each print.

● **Mix colour and black and white** to draw attention to selected areas.

● **Use colour negative film** as a starting point, rather than colour transparencies. Negatives allow you much more control over the colour and density of the finished print, so it is easier to match up each of the elements in the montage.

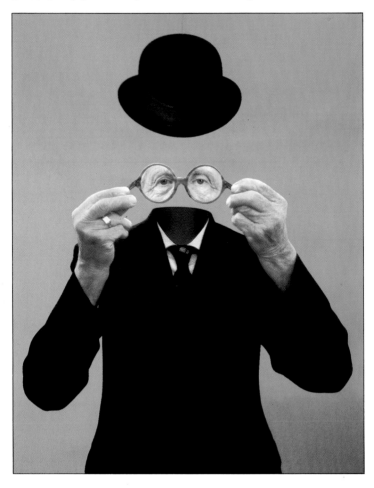

◀ Ideas for surreal montages in colour. There are three elements in the headless man – a hat suspended on a cord, the man's face behind glasses, and his body. The car includes a pale upside-down print.

▶ Two separate pictures – a girl in sunglasses and a car – were taken specifically for this montage suggesting glamorous living.

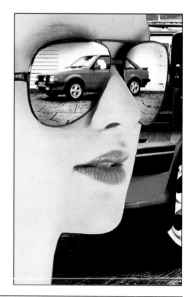

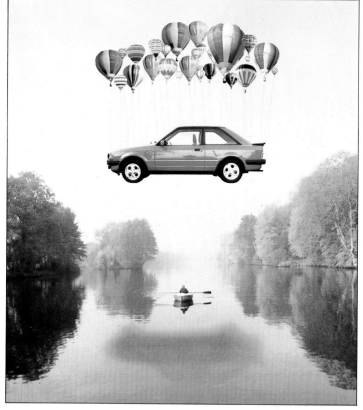

# Montage Patterns

Montage normally involves creating a picture by sticking together different images. Yet one of the attractions of photography is the way you can reproduce the same image again and again. You can exploit this unique ability to create arresting patterns by montaging repeated images. The individual images are best printed separately since this gives the most scope for variation within the pattern. But if your pattern is to be symmetrical, and the idea of making 150 prints is daunting, try the short cut suggested.

● **Plan the pattern** carefully in advance, using graph paper.

● **Print on Grade 5 paper** and maximize contrast – the pattern may not stand out with soft prints.

● **Create a sense of perspective** by 'overlapping' the images – that is, cropping more and more from each successive print.

● **Print 'distant' images lighter** and less contrasty in perspective images, like that below, to enhance the sense of depth.

● **A short cut** in printing the images for symmetrical patterns is to print a few small images, montage them, copy the montage and make as many prints as you need from the copy.

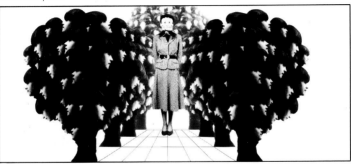

▲ I made this bizarre avenue by making a series of prints of the girl's head, some reversed, some not, and montaging them on artboard. The lines were ruled in ink.

▼ This frieze was created by printing the same shot four times and montaging the prints. By cropping a little more from each print, I created an overlap.

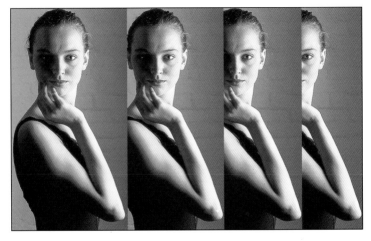

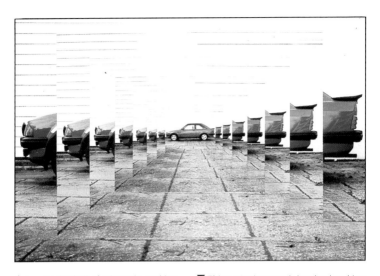

▲ I made this hall of mirrors by making eight prints of the car, of decreasing sizes (the smallest slightly paler). The image was carefully planned to ensure straight perspective lines.

▼ This multiple portrait involved making 121 individual prints of the original image on Grade 5 paper and sticking them all painstakingly on art board and then photographing the result.

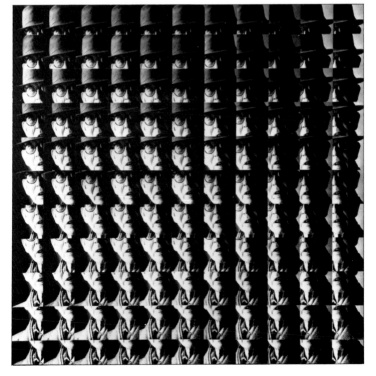

# Combine Techniques

By combining some or all of the techniques outlined in the preceding pages, you can create highly original images or pictures. Montage and airbrush complement one another especially well, for the soft spray of the airbrush helps to blend the most unlikely elements into a colourful and coherent picture.

● **Plan your images** carefully. Photographic materials are expensive, and any waste is costly.

● **Work as large as you can** afford. Large prints and boards are easier to work on, especially for fine detail. Blemishes and mistakes will be disguised when the finished piece is copied and reproduced at a smaller size.

● **Keep the lighting 'realistic',** however dramatic the effect you want. If the lighting looks impossible, the effect will be ruined.

● **Take stock shots** of attractive sunsets, dramatic skies, rising moons and other subjects that may be useful for montages. Remember to keep these shots plain and uncluttered by irrelevant detail.

● **Build up the picture** in stages. Start by printing the background to the right size. Montage the different elements in place. Then, with the aid of masks, create the right finish with an airbrush.

● **Skies darken higher up.** Remember this when airbrushing.

● **Keep the airbrushing subtle.**

● **Photograph** the finished artwork and use the photograph to make a straight print. Put the original safely away. Making a copy print protects the delicate original and helps to disguise traces of your handiwork.

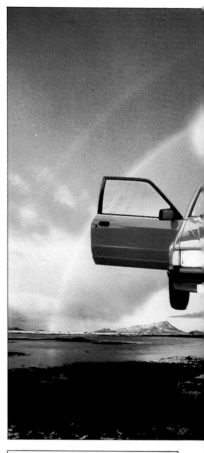

▶ I built up the flying car from three picture elements: a straight shot of a car in soft studio lighting; a landscape including half a rainbow, printed right and wrong way round to make a complete rainbow; and a 'vapour trail' added with an airbrush.

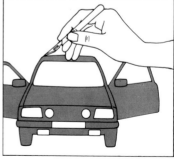

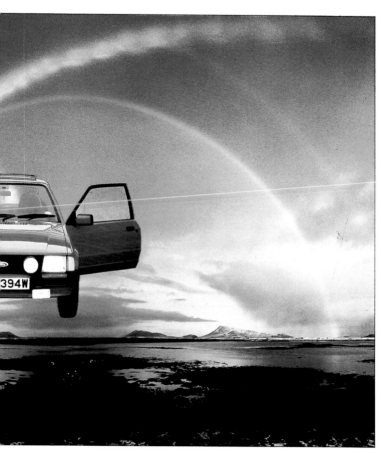

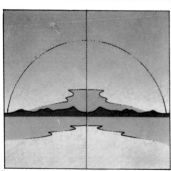

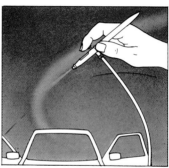

# Retouch Prints

Retouching is one of the most valuable of all darkroom skills. By careful retouching, you can rescue prints blemished by dust spots and scratches, blotchy tones and even unwanted detail. You can also improve the image by bringing up some tones and playing down others. Retouching is not a substitute for proper care in printing and your first task is always to get the best possible print. But, with practice, you can darken or lighten any part of the image you wish to make a print fit for mounting and presentation.

● **Retouch on fibre-based papers** rather than RC papers.

● **Do not handle the print.** Protect it with a sheet of tracing paper.

● **Soak the print** in water to which some wetting solution has been added before bleaching.

● **Lighten large dark areas** by swabbing them with cotton wool soaked in Farmer's reducer. Then wash the print thoroughly.

● **Deal with mistakes immediately** by mopping up with a wet sponge or by washing the whole print.

● **Lighten small areas** with a fibreglass pencil or a small paintbrush filled with reducer.

● **Remove tiny dark spots** by scraping them away with a scalpel blade (see below left).

● **Fill in white spots** on a dry print with a lead pencil or with a fine paintbrush filled with photo-dye or watercolour. Build the colour up in stages until its density is correct (see below right).

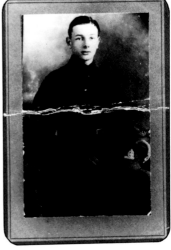

▲ Old prints can often be given a new lease of life with retouching skills, but do not retouch on the original; make a copy first. Not only does this allow for mistakes, it has the advantage that as you make the copy, you may be able to eliminate yellow stains by photographing through a blue filter. The picture above was torn in two when found, so I mounted the two halves on card and photographed it in the enlarger (see page 114).

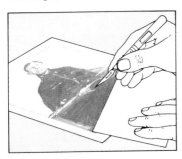

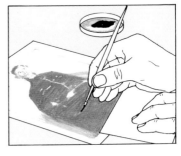

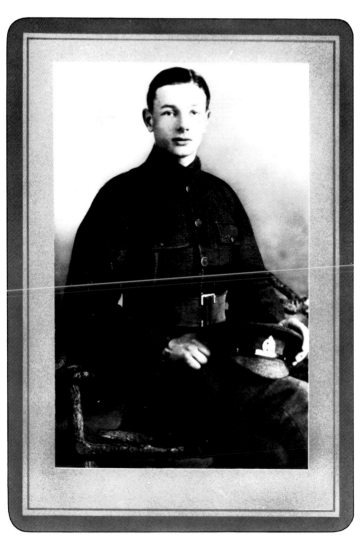

▲ From the copy negative of the torn original, I made a print on unglazed fibre paper and worked on this. Although the final print was in fact to be fairly small, I made this work print on 10 x 8in paper so that any errors would be reduced in size in the final print. All the tiny scratches were disguised by spotting with a fine brush and watercolour paints. The crack across the original was sprayed with an airbrush (see pages 108–9). The background was still blotchy, so I carefully wetted the area and swabbed it with cotton wool soaked in Farmer's reducer to clean it up. I then rephotographed the retouched print and made the final print. This kind of restoration work is well worth doing if you are intent on building up a good historical album. The negatives of many important early photographs have been lost and these images sadly exist now only as damaged or dog-eared prints. Retouching these prints helps to preserve bygone days for those to come.

# Colour by Hand

Colouring black-and-white prints by hand is one of the simplest and cheapest of all darkroom techniques, yet the subtle, pastel hues that can be achieved and the fine control over colour is unmatched. By skilful hand-colouring, you can breathe delicate life into a grey print, highlight different parts of the picture, or create an entirely new image.

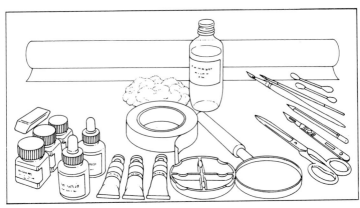

▲ For successful hand-colouring you will need some of these items: rubber masking lacquer; dyes; inks and tubes of colour; a small sponge; a mixing palette; spirit for oils; a magnifier; scissors; a scalpel; a range of brushes; cotton wool; pieces of blotting paper.

● **Make the print** on fibre-based paper, rather than RC. RC prints absorb even watercolours poorly. Use matt paper rather than glossy because large areas of colour may not go on evenly and be blotchy on gloss paper.

● **Underexpose** and underdevelop the print slightly, and print on fairly soft paper – the best prints for hand-colouring are usually rather flat and light since dark tones tend to overwhelm the colour.

● **Sepia-tone prints** in order to give a slightly more natural, warmer look to hand-coloured prints. Or make the print on warmer-toned chlorobromide paper.

● **Use any colouring material** you choose – watercolours, dyes, oil colours, felt tip pens, coloured pencils or even food dyes. Oils do, however, give a more professional look.

● **Use proper photographic dyes** for your first experiments. They will reproduce on film just as they are seen by the eye.

● **For bright, vivid colours,** use water-based retouching dyes.

● **Soak the print well** in water before you apply water-based retouching dyes. Wipe away excess water with a squeegee. Tape down the wet print to prevent it curling as it dries.

● **Dilute the dyes** with plenty of water to give a very weak tint.

● **Colour large areas** with a wide brush or a cotton wool swab, building up the colour gradually layer by layer.

● **Work quickly** so that large areas are not left half-coloured as the print dries.

● **Keep blotting paper to hand** to absorb running colours.

● **Mask adjacent coloured areas** with rubber masking solution.

● **Use finer brushes** and less dilute colours on a dry print for details.

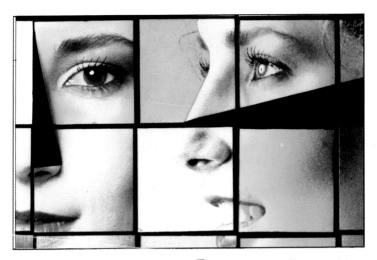

▲ I coloured this print with water-based dyes. Each area was coloured, then masked with rubber solution while colour was applied to new areas.

▼ Hand-colouring is effective at giving a period look to a print – provided the subject is right. Here, watercolours highlight the handcart and milkman.

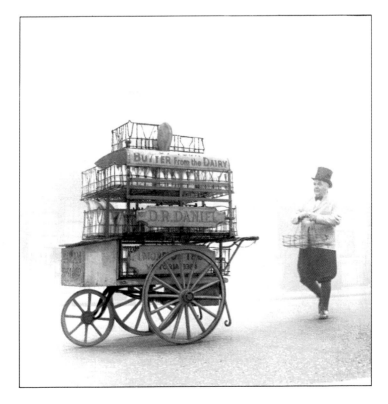

# Use an Airbrush

Airbrushing is a difficult technique, but, once mastered, it allows you to make dramatic changes to prints and to give your montages a slick, professional look. With an airbrush, you can eliminate unwanted backgrounds, add colour where you want, retouch to hide cracks or joins in montages or even create an entirely new picture. An airbrush is basically a spray gun that delivers paint in a fine controllable spray. Some are powered by a compressor, some use just an aerosol can, but both types are used in much the same way.

● **Load the colour** reservoir of the airbrush with a hoghair brush. Use grit-free paint, e.g. gouache.

● **Adjust the air pressure** to suit the paint (follow the makers' instructions).

● **Hold the brush** like a pencil at an angle of 45°. Keep your index finger on the control button.

● **Start to spray** by first pressing the control to start the air flow and then pulling it back to release the colour.

● **Control the spray** by balancing the air and colour flow.

● **Practise on paper** and then on an old print.

● **Spray in parallel strokes** in one direction only, stopping the colour at the end of each stroke.

● **Always use masks** when airbrushing: there is no other way of controlling where colour goes.

● **Remove unwanted colour** in a colour print by airbrushing with white paint and then building up the desired colour on top.

● **Protect** delicate airbrushed prints by rephotographing them (see page 114).

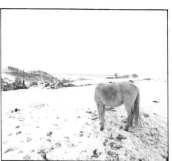

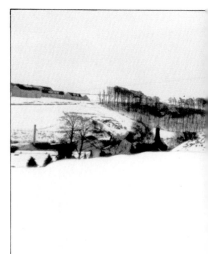

▲ In the original 35mm transparency of the hose, the snow around was well-trampled and unattractive. I made a 8 x 10in colour negative and then deleted the entire snow area with black dye. On a positive of the same size, I then airbrushed in the unblemished snow.

▶ The final print both emphasizes the horse's shape and creates a minor mystery – how did the horse get there in the first place when there are no hoofprints in the surrounding snow?

▶ To remove detail from a large and complex area of a print, you must use an adhesive mask. Lay the film for the mask over the entire print and its mount. With a sharp, new scalpel blade, carefully cut through the film around the area you want to spray. Be very careful to avoid cutting the print as well. When cutting round dark areas, err a little on the dark side of the tone boundary or you will get a 'halo' effect. Once you have cut out the area to be sprayed, peel the film away carefully. You are now ready to start airbrushing. Start by spraying the area evenly in a colour that matches the surrounding area. Build up the colour in smooth strokes, overlapping half of the stroke each time. Be very sparing in your use of colour. If in doubt, spray thinly, wait until it dries, and go over the area again. When you have an even tone, you can begin to add detail if you wish. In skies, for instance, you could add white, fluffy clouds. Practise the effect on waste paper first, though.

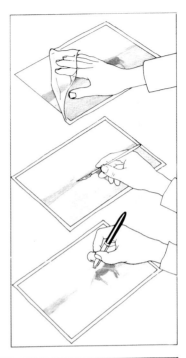

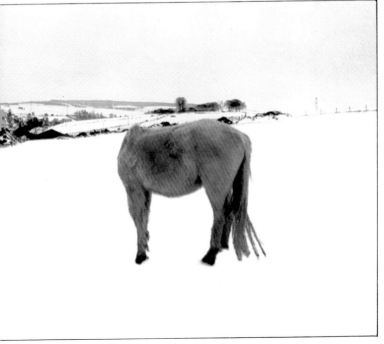

# Tone Black-and-White Prints

Toners enable you to add colour or mood to a black-and-white print. The best known is sepia, which lends prints an air of antiquity; blue toner gives them the chill of winter. You can extend the technique to produce multi-coloured prints in which the colours ca n be as true or as creatively unnatural as you care to make them. Most toners are readily available in ready-to-use packs.

## Sepia toning

Toning with sepia gives prints a rich brown colour and makes them more stable and permanent.

● **Make sure** that the room is adequately ventilated: sodium sulphide toner is very smelly and can be toxic. Thiocarbamide toners are less noisome, and can be more flexible.

● **Use fibre-based papers** for prints you intend to sepia tone. The process softens contrast and brings out shadow detail, so adjust printing to suit it.

● **Soak dry prints** in water for half an hour before toning.

● **Immerse the print** in a bleaching solution of potassium ferricyanide and potassium bromide until the black metallic silver of the image has changed to pale yellow silver bromide.

● **Wash the print** for about five minutes until all traces of yellow have disappeared.

● **Filter the water** for the toner if it contains impurities.

● **Immerse the print** in the toning solution, rocking the dish continuously until you cannot see any further change in colour.

● **Wash the print** for ten minutes in running water.

● **Dispose** of the toning solution down an outside drain.

## Blue toning

Iron toning, a process which consists of converting the metallic silver on the print to a ferrocyanide salt, gives a dark blue-toned print.

● **Use resin-coated paper.**

● **Underexpose the print** a stop so that the toner brings it up to normal intensity.

● **Make the toning bath** from two stock solutions. Mix them without dilution before use.

● **Prewash the print** for an hour.

● **Use a hypo clearer** to make sure that the print is clean.

● **Immerse the print** in the toning solution and rock the dish until the desired depth of tone is achieved.

● **Wash the print** for about three to four minutes.

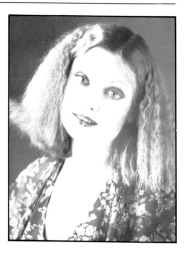

▲ This print was made by bleaching a black-and-white print and redarkening it in a blue toner. Blue toners generally darken and intensify the print, so the original print was deliberately underexposed and underdeveloped.

### Dye coupler toning

Dye coupler toning exploits colour chemistry to colour black-and-white prints. It involves bleaching the silver print image back to the original silver halides, then redeveloping it in colour developer. Special colour couplers are added to the developer: these 'couple' coloured dyes to the silver so that it is combined with a dye image.

● **Soak the print well.**

● **Bleach** in standard bleach, then wash for ten minutes.

● **Mix the colour developer** and add the chosen coupler.

● **Immediately develop** the print until the colour is right.

● **Rinse thoroughly.**

● **Briefly stabilize** the print.

▼ A mixture of yellow and cyan colour couplers was used to produce this dye-coupled print. The second bleach-fix bath, which removes the silver, leaving only the dye, was omitted in order to give the picture a fuller image.

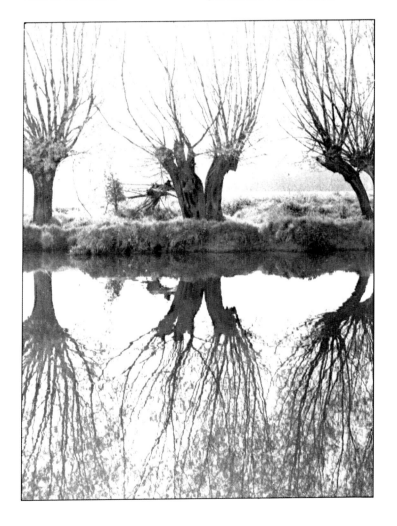

# Print on any Surface

With the aid of liquid emulsion, you can print photographs onto virtually any surface you choose. You can print pictures on plates, blocks of wood, stones, eggs – almost anything small enough to fit in your darkroom. Liquid emulsion, available in kit form, is simply painted onto the surface under safelight, exposed and processed normally. A number of different liquid emulsions are available from specialist darkroom outlets.

● **Choose an image** to match the surface. A picture of a chicken might go on an egg, and so on.

● **Analyse the surface** you wish to print on. All surfaces need preparation, and some may need 'subbing' before they can be coated with emulsion.

● **Prepare non-porous surfaces,** such as glass and glazed ceramics, by first cleaning very thoroughly with hot washing soda, then 'sub' them with a 5 per cent gelatin solution, warmed in a bowl of water until it goes on easily.

● **Prepare cloth and paper** by cleaning thoroughly to remove any traces of chemicals.

● **Coat the back of paper** with a 5 per cent gelatin solution: this will prevent it curling.

● **Seal wood, clay** and other porous surfaces with a polyurethane varnish to stop the emulsion soaking in unevenly.

● **Seal surfaces** that might react with the emulsion by coating them with polyurethane varnish. This includes metal surfaces containing brass or iron.

● **Do not be dismayed** if the first attempt does not work: this is one of the most fickle of darkroom processes, especially on surfaces like glass.

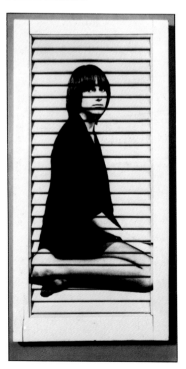

◀ At first sight, printing directly onto such a large surface as this louvred door seemed to be a daunting task. But in the event it proved to be quite straightforward, since I was able to take the door off its hinges and carry it to the darkroom to work on. The surface needed no preparation apart from thorough cleaning, for the paintwork provided a perfect subbing layer. I tilted the enlarger head to give a large enough image and focused on a piece of old print paper taped to the door. I then coated a few small strips of similarly painted wood with liquid emulsion under safelight and made a few test exposures. With the exposure time established, I sensitized the door by filling a household plant spray with liquid emulsion and sprayed it over the surface. I then made the exposure and processed the image by swabbing the door down with a sponge soaked with all the chemicals in turn. An old plastic washing-up bowl made an ideal 'developing tray' for this and neatly caught all the drips.

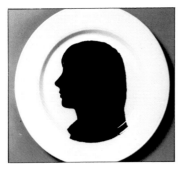

◀ With liquid emulsions, you can make your own personalized plates. Printing on a plate can be almost as easy as making a normal black-and-white print, for the surface is flat, and many printing plates will slip into standard processing trays for processing. But, as with all ceramics, the surface must be properly 'subbed' by soaking it in 5 per cent gelatin solution, warmed in water, before you coat the plate with the liquid emulsion.

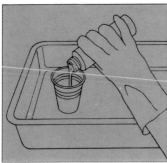

**1** Melt the emulsion by placing your storage bottle in a hot water bath – not over direct heat. You will have to judge the quantity you need to cover the plate. Try to avoid pouring too much – it is expensive, and you may fog any emulsion returned to the bottle.

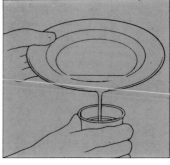

**2** Pour the emulsion onto the warmed plate. Use rubber gloves to hold the plate. Spread your hand over the underside to avoid thumb marks, and roll the emulsion around to get an even coating. Work quickly in case the emulsion coagulates.

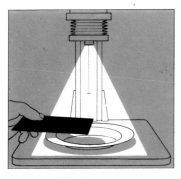

**3** Liquid emulsion is easy to remove by washing in hot water and scrubbing gently, so you can make a series of test exposures on the plate in the same way as prints on paper. Once you know the correct exposure, wash off, recoat the plate and make the full print.

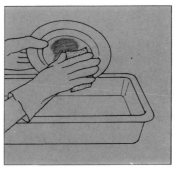

**4** Process the plate as you would a print. You will need to extend the fixing time, using an acid-hardened fixer. Handle the plate carefully as the emulsion will remain soft until thoroughly dry. Wash very gently in tepid water. Finally, dry off and varnish with polyurethane.

# Copy Pictures

An enlarger makes a wonderfully versatile and high-quality copying machine, and it is well worth learning how to exploit it as a copier, for copying is an integral part of many advanced darkroom techniques. Enlargers can be used for three main copying procedures, although not all enlargers are equally suitable for each. First, and most significantly, the enlarger can be used to copy negatives and slides onto sheet films in much the same way as for printing onto paper. Second, it can be used as a copy camera to photograph flat artwork, such as completed montages. Third, it can be used, in conjunction with a camera, to make high-quality duplicates of slides.

**Copying onto sheet film**

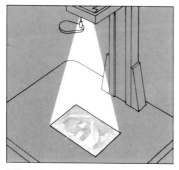

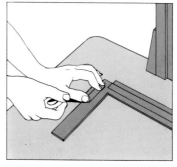

**1** Place the slide or negative to be copied in the enlarger negative carrier and compose and focus the image as for normal printing (page 52). The size depends on the size of the sheet film – typically 5 x 4in.

**2** Mark the edge of the image on the enlarger baseboard – the easel may be awkward to use – and then tape strips of black card down to make stops against which you can register the film in complete darkness.

**Flat copying**

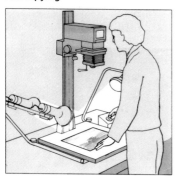

▲ Some enlargers are especially designed for easy transformation into copy cameras. This one has a reflex focusing screen, a film carrier that takes 35mm film in a light-tight package, and a copy stand equipped with lights.

● **Use the focusing screen** if your enlarger has one. Otherwise...

● **Focus** by projecting a negative onto the baseboard the same size as the image you wish to copy.

● **Use the film carrier** if your enlarger has one. Otherwise ...

● **Place a sheet of film,** bigger than the negative masks, in the negative carrier in darkness. Seal the carrier with opaque tape.

● **Light the image either** with proper copying lights, or by moving a lamp held at an angle of 45° across the surface during the exposure.

**Calculate the necessary exposure** from tests.

● **Use the masks** in the negative carrier to cut down flare. This is more important with copying than with printing.

● **Use black paper** under the film during exposure if the baseboard of your enlarger is white. Reflection from the baseboard can cause halation.

● **Do not handle the film** any more than is absolutely necessary.

● **Make sure** that the emulsion is at the top when you place the sheet of film under the enlarger.

● **Tape the register stops** to make sure that the film cannot slip underneath.

● **Copies on colour sheet film** can be made in exactly the same way, but you must work in total darkness and take much greater care.

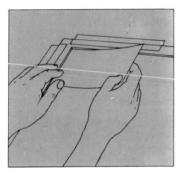

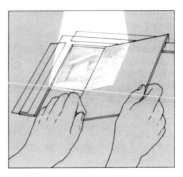

**3** Under safelight, if you are using orthochromatic film, or in total darkness if you are using panchromatic film to make copies from colour originals, slide the sheet film against the card, with the notch bottom left.

**4** Make a series of test exposures in exactly the same way as for ordinary black-and-white prints. Process in a colour print drum. Find the correct exposure and repeat the procedure to make the full copy.

### Duplicating slides

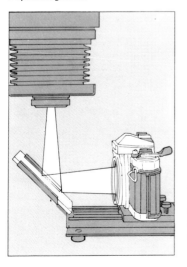

● **The simplest way** to duplicate slides using an enlarger is to remove the lens from a 35mm SLR and place the camera under the enlarger. The slide is then projected in the enlarger directly into the aperture of the SLR. Unfortunately, since you cannot use the camera viewfinder, it is difficult to compose the image.

● **The best arrangement** is with a front-silvered mirror held at an angle of 45° beneath the lens to reflect the image into the camera. Purpose-built stands with a rigid bracket for the camera are available.

● **Use filters** or the dial-in colour head of the enlarger in order to control the colour of the light.

# Work in Register

Many darkroom techniques involve separating an image into various elements – tone separations, colour separations, contrast masks and many others. These elements are then reunited for the final print. If the image is to look sharp, the elements must be perfectly aligned. It is possible to 'register' the images visually in good light, but in dim light or total darkness it is impossible.

● **The best method** of registration is with a punch system. This involves making two or more holes near the edge of each sheet of film or paper, in exactly the same place. The images are registered by slotting the holes over corresponding pins.

● **Register separations** made from a single negative onto sheet film under the enlarger by punching holes in each sheet before exposure. Tape a set of register pins to the enlarger baseboard and locate the film on the pins for each exposure.

● **Keep contact copies registered** over a complex sequence of copying and recopying by using a contact printer equipped with register pins. Punch register holes in each new sheet of film or paper.

● **The cheapest punch** register system is a good-quality office punch inlaid into a wooden board to allow the film to slide level into the jaws of the punch. Make register pins with wooden dowelling rod. These can be taped to a bar for use under the enlarger or used in a contact printer.

● **Photographic punch register** systems such as Kodak's will ensure greater precision than possible with a home-made system.

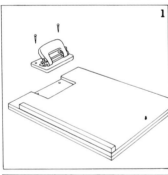

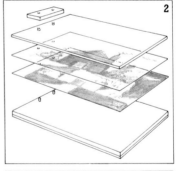

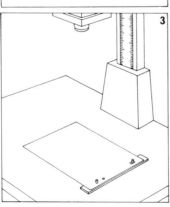

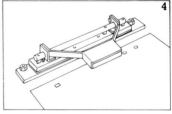

1. Home-made registration board
2. Registered contact print
3. Registering separations under the enlarger
4. Kodak punch system

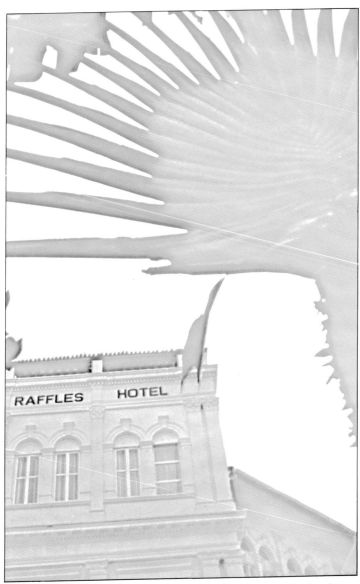

▲ Many of the more spectacular darkroom effects depend on working in register. This colourful view of the Raffles Hotel in Singapore was created by first printing the original slide onto neg/pos paper to give an image reversed in both tone and colour. I then punched this print and a second sheet of unexposed paper with register holes and laid them in a contact printer in complete darkness. I switched on the enlarger to expose the second sheet (since the exposure was through print paper, the exposure needed to be 20 times as long as it would normally be). I then sandwiched both prints together in register and contact printed onto a third sheet.

# Make Colour Separations

Colour separation is an essential feature of many advanced darkroom manipulations, and it is worth spending some time learning the technique. Colour separation involves splitting the colour image into its blue, green and red components by making three copies on black-and-white film through blue, green and red filters respectively.

● **Start with any original** – artwork, flat copy, colour slide or colour negative. But if you start with a colour negative make a normal print and work from this.

● **Work from a colour slide** if you can; it is much easier. Photograph artwork and flat copy onto slide film if necessary.

● **Include a grey scale** in the picture if you take it specifically for colour separation. It makes exposure calculation and colour balance much easier.

● **Use panchromatic black-and-white film** for the separations. This means working in total darkness at times, for there is no safelight for panchromatic films, but it must be panchromatic to record tones for all the colours of the original. On orthochromatic film, reds would not be recorded.

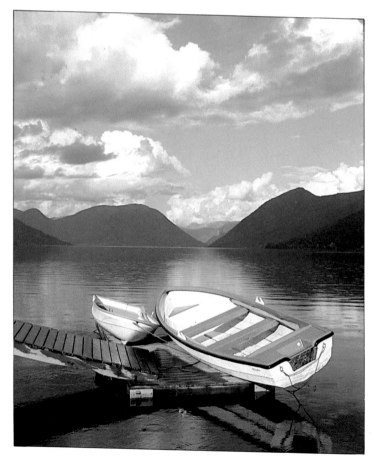

● **Work with sheet film** – 5 x 4in is ideal – unless you specifically want 35mm copies. Separations on sheet film are easier to work with.

● **Use narrow cut filters** to ensure complete separation. An ideal separation set is the Wratten filters 29, 61 and 47B.

● **Make separations on sheet film** by projecting the slide in the enlarger in exactly the same way as for ordinary prints.

● **Register each sheet** using a register bar taped to the enlarger baseboard (see page 116).

● **Cut the corners** to help identify each separation.

● **Start exposure tests** for each negative with the following exposures if you are using the Wratten filter set suggested and enlarging 35mm originals onto 5 x 4in. With the lens set at *f*8, expose through the blue filter for 25 seconds, the green for 15 seconds and the red for 30.

● **Process the separations** in trays as recommended. Develop all three negatives together, but leave the red and green separations in for 4½ minutes and the blue for 7 for uniform contrast.

▼ Separations from colour slides give three separation negatives. If you need positives, simply make contact prints on sheet film.

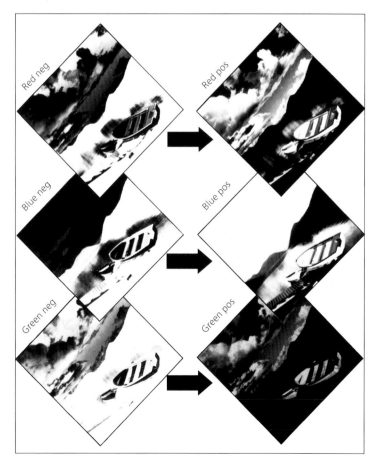

# Posterize Prints

With a technique called posterization you can create a print in bold, striking colours, like a poster, from any original, whether colour or black and white. It involves making a series of tone separations on black-and-white film, then printing them in register through colour filters onto colour print paper in any combination you wish. The result depends entirely on the filters chosen.

● **Copy colour originals** onto ordinary black-and-white film. Black-and-white negatives can be used directly.

● **Make tone separations** from the black-and-white copy by printing from it onto three sheets of lith film, exposing one print normally, underexposing one by 1½ stops and overexposing the third by 1½ stops.

● **Choose the size** of the lith film sheets according to the size of print you

want, unless you are lucky enough to have an enlarger capable of printing from large sheets of film.

● **Ensure perfect register** by taping a peg-bar onto the enlarger baseboard and punching register holes in each sheet of film. For register techniques see page 116.

● **Contact print** each separation onto lith film again so that you have three negative and three positive separations.

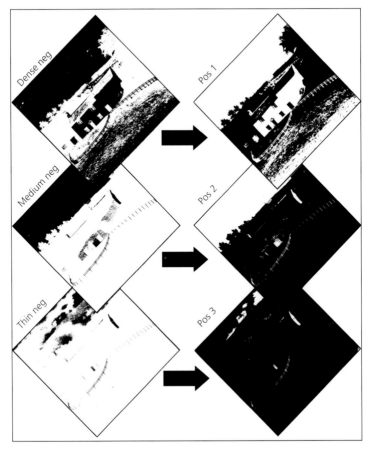

● **Number each** colour or tone separation so that you can repeat the print.

● **Make a posterized print** by contact printing (or enlarging) the separations onto black-and-white or colour print paper.

● **For black-and-white** posterizations, simply print all three separations in sequence onto black-and-white paper, giving only enough exposure to each separation to produce a mid-grey tone in the shadows.

● **For the simplest of colour** posterizations, expose a single separation onto colour print paper with a coloured light source.

● **For multi-coloured** posterizations you should print various combinations of separations onto colour print paper, using a differently coloured light for each exposure.

● **Colour the light** by placing different coloured filters under the enlarger or in the enlarger filter drawer.

▼ The posterized image of the house was created by making three tone separations of varying density from the original transparency, then contact printing each onto high-contrast lith film. These films were then contacted back to positives and then printed down in combination, using different light sources.

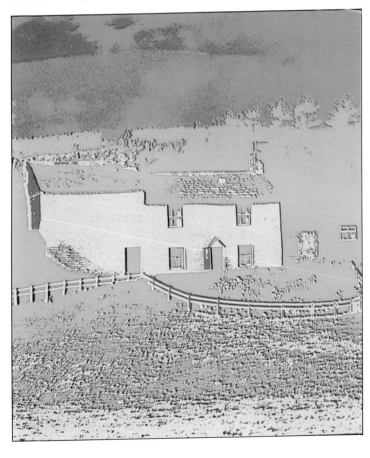

# Create Negative Images

Using one of the simplest darkroom techniques, it is easy to create striking, imaginative imagery. A deliberate mismatch of film and paper or chemistry produces tonal and colour reversals. For example, printing a colour transparency onto monochrome paper produces a black-and-white negative image similar to those shown below. Printing slides onto colour negative paper provides even greater potential for creative manipulation. Cross-processing takes this technique a step further: for bizarre, high-contrast effects try processing slide film in C-41 colour negative chemistry.

● **Print slides** onto monochrome paper for simple tonal reversal. Transparencies have much higher contrast than black-and-white negatives, so if you want a full tonal range, you will need to print on a soft grade of paper such as Grade 0 or 1. However, higher-than-normal contrast may even improve the picture.

● **Make prints from prints** by pressing an existing monochrome print in contact with a fresh sheet of paper. Use a sheet of glass to hold the sandwich together, then make a contact print as if you were proofing a whole roll of film, as explained on pages 46–49. After processing, the new print will have its tones reversed.

● **Process slides as negatives** to produce high contrast and distorted colours. For best results, expose the film at double the recommended speed.

● **Process negatives in E-6** (reversal) chemistry only if you want a very low-contrast effect, and have time to spend printing. The film's yellow masking layer hides many of the colours of the resulting slides.

● **Reverse the hues of slides** by printing them on colour negative paper. The slide lacks a negative's yellow masking layer, so prints will have very warm tones. You can avoid this by sandwiching a piece of processed, but unexposed, colour negative film in the carrier along with the slide.

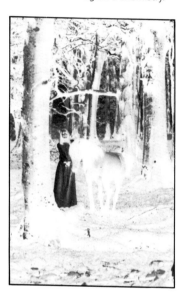

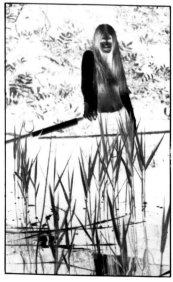

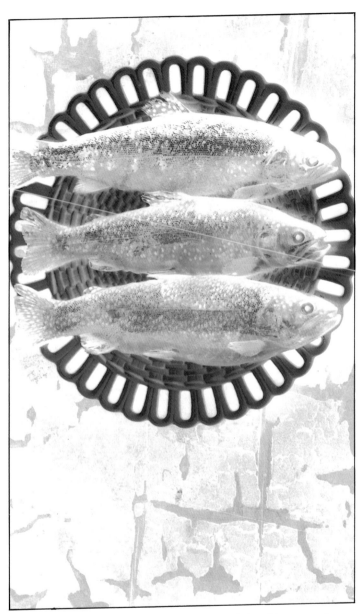

◄ Printing slides onto monochrome paper turns day to night. For both of these images, I printed an Ektachrome transparency onto Multigrade paper, using a number ½ filter to keep the contrast down.

▲ When printing slides on negative paper, do not be too concerned with the conventional rules about colour. I experimented with a number of different filtrations before settling on this blue-green image.

# Mask for Contrast

Contrast masking is a technique for increasing or reducing contrast, especially in slides, with a degree of accuracy impossible with dodging and burning in masks. But it is also an interesting way of producing false colour images. The technique involves printing the original in contact with a thin, underexposed black-and-white copy onto colour reversal paper.

● **Decide** whether you want a sharp mask or an unsharp mask. Both are produced in the same way – by making a contact from the original – but an unsharp mask is made by separating the two emulsions with a diffusing sheet. The unsharp mask is more usual and ensures that slight errors of registration are not noticeable.

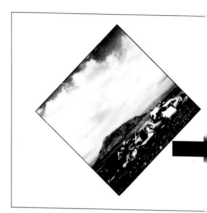

**To reduce contrast:**
● **Make an unsharp mask** by exposing special masking film or, if that is impossible, ordinary black-and-white film in contact with the original.

● **Experiment with exposure** and development until you have a very thin, flat negative with little or no image in the highlight areas.

**To increase contrast:**
● **Use separation negative film** to make a sharp (emulsion to emulsion) internegative from the original slide.

● **Experiment with exposure** and development until you have a crisp, detailed image.

● **Sandwich the interneg** with another piece of the same film in register, and give a short exposure to produce an underexposed image with no detail in the highlights.

**To print with masks:**
● **Sandwich the mask** you need in register with the original. When printing, increase exposure to allow for the density of the mask.

**To alter colour:**
● **Sandwich** the colour negative or transparency with a negative or positive contrast mask and expose with a coloured light source. Or use both masks, and a double exposure.

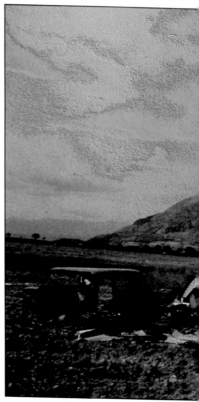

▼ The two contrast masks below were used in a double exposure to make the picture of a car cemetery. The first exposure was for the original transparency sandwiched with an underexposed contrast mask; the second for the transparency was sandwiched with the positive of the mask. By using different colour light sources for each exposure, the division between the highlights and the rest of the image was enhanced.

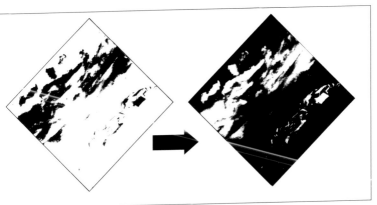

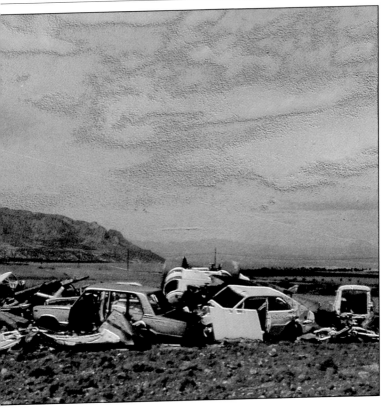

# Create a Mandala

A mandala is a motif arranged in the form of a repeated pattern, rather like a Rorsach inkblot or the mirror-image of a kaleidoscope. Photographic mandalas can have graphic design applications for wallpapers and textiles, and you can make powerful and intriguing mandalas by such techniques as photomontage, multiple printing or – as in the example below – by combining duplicate slides.

● **Choose an image** of a regular, uniform shape that lends itself well to repetition. For a colour mandala, photograph it on slide film. For a black-and-white mandala, make a contact positive.

● **Shoot an existing object,** for example, an abstract detail against a plain background or a greatly magnified fragment shot with a macro lens. The mandala here was based on a crankshaft.

● **Look through** your stock shots to find a suitable image. Pictures with bold diagonals and converging lines and broad, simple shapes are ideal.

● **Isolate sections** of posterized, solarized and prism-filter images. Do not overlook your black-and-white prints. High-contrast images, silhouettes, and pictures shot on lith film make strong patterns and motifs of considerable impact.

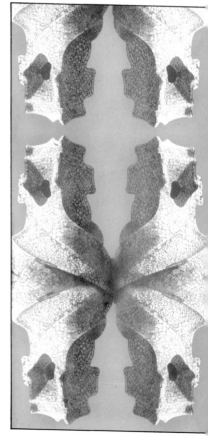

▶ The mandala on the right was made with 18 duplicates of the original slide on Kodak 5071 copying film. After making the duplicates, I drew up a grid on tracing paper using a slide to determine the size of the grid squares and taped this over a lightbox (above). I then carefully cut away the borders of the slides, using a sharp scalpel and a metal straight-edge. With a fine brush, I placed a bare minimum of glue along the edge of each slide and stuck the slides together over the grid, waiting for the glue to set on each join before adding the next slide.

● **Make copies** of your original, some with the image the right way round, some with the image reversed.

● **Reverse the image** simply by 'flopping' the film over and exposing through the front.

● **Make duplicate slides** if you want to make a series of copies of your finished mandala. Sticking slides together accurately requires considerable skill, but you will be able to use the finished mandala to make any number of copies by contact printing. Copies on 35mm film may also be relatively cheap to make.

● **Copy onto 5 x 4in film** if you only want a few images in your mandala.

This will be more expensive, but the large slides are much easier to work with and give a bigger print.

● **Join slides** by drawing a grid for the images onto tracing paper, taping this to a lightbox and laying the slides on this. Trim the slides to mate exactly, with a scalpel and a metal rule, and stick them together by lightly brushing the film edges with clear adhesive, making sure that the slides do not stick to the paper.

● **Montage prints of the original** if you feel joining slides is too tricky, then photograph the result. Or make a series of exposures onto the same sheet of paper, using masks and a pre-drawn grid to establish positions.

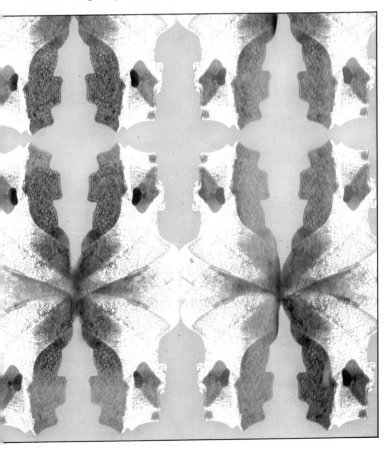

# Exploit Neons

A sheet of opalescent material is commonly used to provide an even light source for viewing and projecting film. You can also use it to create spectacular haloes like neon lights around an image. The effect, called neoning, depends on the way the sheet scatters light and works in the same way as the corona in a total eclipse. The idea is to make a negative silhouette and a positive. The neon is created by sandwiching the sheet and plate glass between the negative and positive, and illuminating the negative from behind. Without the opalescence, the positive silhouette would block all light coming through the negative mask. With the sheet, just enough light is scattered to create a brilliant outline.

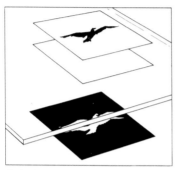

▲ The lith positive was photographed against a blue light, then by taping the negative underneath an opalescent sheet and glass and illuminating it with yellow light to create a neon for a second exposure.

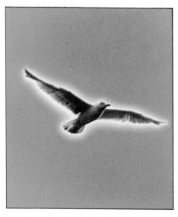

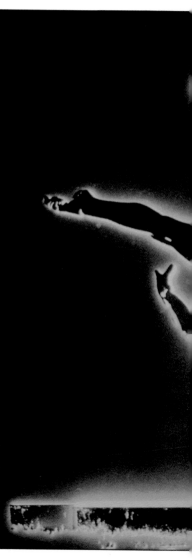

▶ For this picture I made three flash exposures of a gymnast, copied the negatives onto lith film, and contacted the copies onto lith to make negative and positive masks. Using a green light, I then shot a neon of each on the same frame.

● **Use any original,** providing it has a strong, simple outline.

● **Copy onto lith film** to create a negative mask. Retouch to enhance the silhouette.

● **Contact print the light copy** onto lith to make the positive.

● **Tape the negative** onto a sheet of thick plate glass.

● **Tape the opal film** to the other side of the glass. Use tracing paper if you have no opal film.

● **Register the positive** carefully over the negative and tape down.

● **Illuminate the negative** from underneath. Colour the light with filters if you wish.

● **Photograph from above.**

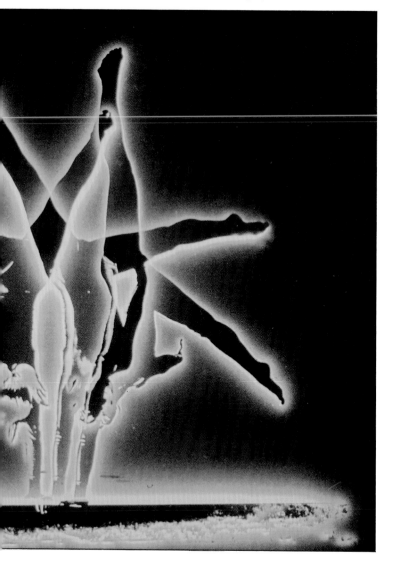

# Computer Montage

Photographers are using computers to create special effects which used to take months to master in the darkroom. With a reasonably powerful PC, a scanner and image manipulation software a print or slide can be turned into a digital image which can be manipulated on screen. You can tone and tint, change contrast, sharpness and graininess. You can also remove unwanted areas, or combine two or more images together. Results are possible in a few seconds, and if you do not like what you see you can go back a single stage – without having to start from the very beginning.

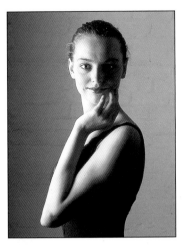

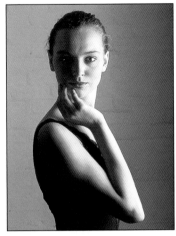

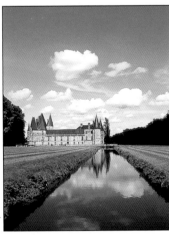

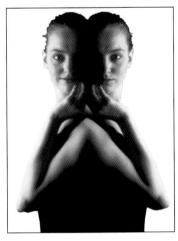

▶ The picture on the right started as two digital images – a portrait shot in the studio, and a shot of a French château. The girl was cut away from the background, and a copy flipped to create a mirror image. These were combined to make the centrepiece for the final image. The background came from the sky from the landscape and cut away from the image of the château. The cuboids were drawn on the computer, with final shading added.

● **For convincing montages,** light the different elements in a similar way.

● **The colour balance** of each element should be adjusted, as necessary, so that they go together well.

● **Sharpness can be adjusted** on each element to make one stand out.

● **Save the working image** as you go along, using different file names, so that you can always go back a step or two should you make a mistake.

● **Images can be scanned** into digital form for you by many high street outlets – and then output onto film or paper when you have finished.

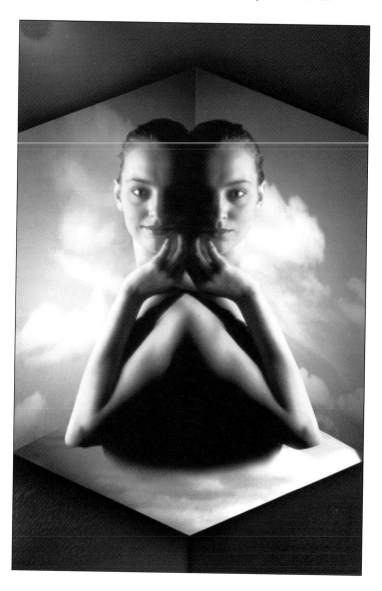

# Computer Retouching

Although the computer can be used to create pictures that bear only a passing resemblance to the original they were sourced from, the main use for manipulation is for more subtle effects. Practically every advertising shot and magazine cover you see today has been altered in some way. A shot of a model on a magazine, for instance, will have had the teeth and eyes whitened, and the colour of the lips enhanced – so that the magazine looks more eye-catching. These subtle changes are unnoticeable to the viewer, but are key to the charm of computer manipulation.

▼ This sequence shows you how easy it is to change the colour of one element of a photograph without affecting the background. You can define an area to be changed yourself, or you can just click on an area and it can be automatically selected. Once this is done, thousands of different colour permutations can be chosen using a colour palette or by entering a colour reference value.

● **Simple blemishes** on a photograph, such as an air bubble or scratch can easily be removed simply by copying minute neighbouring areas over the offending spots. Individual pixels (the elemental squares of colour which make up a picture) can be changed.

● **Back up work** after a long session onto a separate disk – just in case the computer should crash.

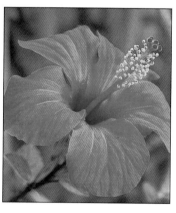

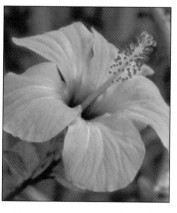

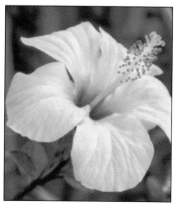

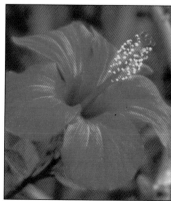

● **A range of colour and darkness** on variations can often be previewed in an individual screen. With an appearance of a darkroom ring-around chart (see pages 78–9), this can help you to spot the best colour balance quickly.

● **Individual colours** of an object can be completely changed, while retaining the original areas of highlight and shadow. This effect works best if the original area contains a good range of mid-tones.

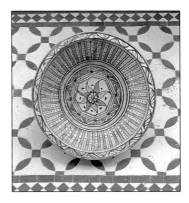

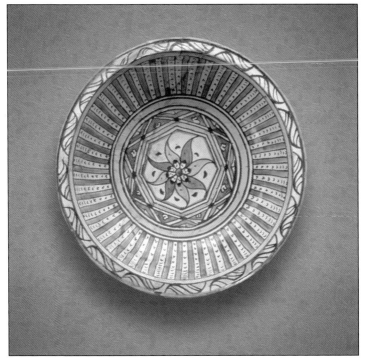

▲ I originally shot this beautiful Moroccan bowl against a tile floor which mimicked elements of its design and colour. However, on later reflection, the two patterns compete for the viewer's attention, so I decided to remove the background on the computer using image manipulation software. I chose a neutral-coloured texture that would allow the colours of the bowl to be seen properly – in this case, a warm, brown tone. To ensure that the result was not too flat, I applied a radial graduated tint to the background – creating shadows in the corners of the frame. Finally, I replaced the shadow below the bowl itself – putting it in the same position, and at the same size as it had appeared in my original, less successful photograph.

# Mount your Prints

Your favourite shots deserve to be properly displayed, and you owe it to yourself to see that the prints are shown off to best advantage, whether at home or at an exhibition of photographs. Make sure that your prints are spotless and carefully retouched where necessary. It is not essential to frame your pictures, but mounts and supports should be thick enough to prevent prints from warping and buckling. Cut-out mounts, preferably of a neutral tone or plain white, will considerably enhance even your best shots, and although thick mounting board is expensive, the investment will be worthwhile. You can buy ready-cut mounts, with matching glass and clips. DIY kit frames are also available in a wide range of standard sizes.

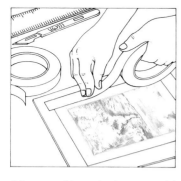

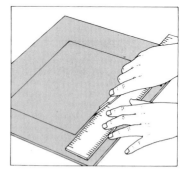

**1** Use a pencil to mark where your print is to be placed on the mounting board. Leave space for the borders. Align the print and attach it to the board by taping the underside and the print and peeling away the release paper.

**2** Measure the window area on your covering mounting board according to the size of your print and mark the rectangle lightly with a pencil. Cut out with a sharp scalpel, slanting to cut a bevel. Watch that you do not overrun the corners. Erase any pencil marks.

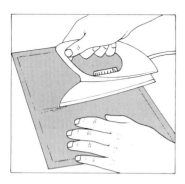

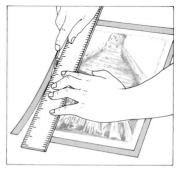

**1** Alternatively, place the print face down and lay the tissue over the back. Gently tack down with the tip of a domestic iron on a low setting. If it fails to melt the glue, increase the heat. Start in the middle and work out, but do not tack the corners.

**2** Now turn the print over and trim away any surplus tissue, or trim both print and tissue together, with a sharp knife. The edges must be flush to avoid the tissue appearing around the outside of the print, unless you intend to cover it with a window mount.

● **Cutting a mount.** The borders of a mount should be of a generous width, the bottom border deeper than the top and sides. With thick card, cut the window mount on a bevel and to the same overall dimensions as the border.

● **Wet and dry mounting.** The simplest technique is to use an adhesive such as latex, applied with a spreader, or an aerosol of spray adhesive.

● **Alternatives include** double-sided adhesive film, where you pull off a back and front release paper, and dry mounting tissue, perhaps the most effective way.

● **Dry mounting tissue** is impregnated with glue which melts when ironed to form a firm bond between print and mount. You can use a domestic flat iron as described below.

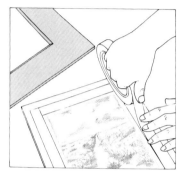

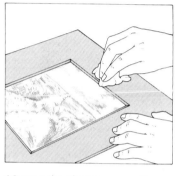

**3** Use double-sided tape along the edges of the print to sandwich the two boards together. Excess rebate on the window mount can be trimmed away with the knife. If you intend to frame your picture, check that the frame section will accept two boards plus glass.

**4** Remove the release papers on the tape, align the two mounting boards and press firmly together. Use a lint-free cloth to avoid leaving finger marks on the mount. A firmer bond between print and support can be made with dry mounting tissue.

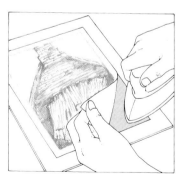

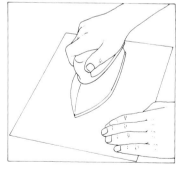

**3** Position the print on the supporting mount, and square to the edges of it, having marked the position with a pencil and ruler. Keep the print in position while you lift each corner in turn, and tack the tissue to the board with the iron.

**4** You now need to protect the face of your print with smooth, unwaxed paper. Heavy brown wrapping paper is ideal. Adjust the iron to a low setting and apply firm pressure to the print, working outwards from the centre. Check that the tissue is bonding.

# Store Film Images

No photographic images last forever. Colour photographs in particular are prone to fading. But you can extend their life considerably by storing them in the right conditions. Proper, organized storage will also help you to find the image you want with minimal fuss. This, in turn, helps to preserve your pictures, for nothing reduces the life of film more than handling.

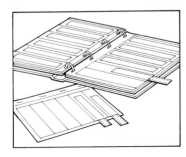 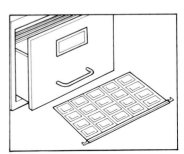

▲ Negative file sheets make a neat way of storing negatives. Slide display sleeves, often known as 'viewpacks', are a convenient and attractive way of storing slides.

● **Always store all films** in dry conditions. Any dampness that is in the air will be taken up by the film very rapidly, softening the emulsion and laying it open to attack.

● **Include a sachet** of silica gel in your storage cabinet or bag to absorb any moisture in the atmosphere, particularly when storing colour film.

● **Avoid dust and grit** like the plague. Make sure your storage cabinet is free from dust, and clean film prior to storage with an antistatic brush.

● **Keep the film cool.** Film will last virtually forever in a dry refrigerator.

● **Store film in darkness.** Colour film fades rapidly in bright light, particularly sunlight and fluorescent light.

● **Never handle films** more than necessary. Refer to the contact sheets or duplicates if you can.

● **Store negatives** on negative file sheets that can be filed neatly away in a series of ring-binders.

● **Store slides** in clear plastic display sleeves if you have only a small collection, or use them for your most cherished or most used slides. They are expensive, but protect each slide in its own individual pocket and allow you to view up to 24 slides at a time without ever touching them. Some versions file neatly into ring-binders and some file into the rack draw of a filing cabinet. As with negatives, you should use polythene, not PVC, sleeves.

● **Store** large slide collections in specially designed storage boxes with slots for individual slides.

● **Store** complete slide shows in magazines ready to load straight into the projector. Bear in mind that magazines for some projectors can be very expensive.

● **Use paper file sheets** if you rarely need to look at the negatives. Special acid-free paper does not react with the film.

● **Use clear plastic sheets** if you need to look at the negatives often. You can see the images clearly without removing the film from its sleeve. But bear in mind that some clear plastics give off vapours that may attack the film if you use clear plastic sleeves; use polythene sleeves instead.

# Project Slides

Unlike prints, slides can only be seen properly by projection. Yet photographers who put considerable effort into getting high-quality slides, will often undermine the value of their work by casual slide projection. To show your slides off to best effect, you should put as much care into projection as any other stage.

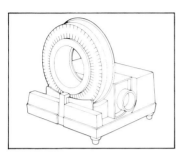
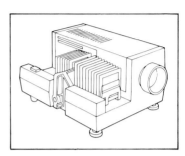

● **Black out the room** as well as you can. Any light leaks will make the richest colours pale and washed out. The brightness of the slide projector light will not compensate for a bright room.

● **Black out the projector** as well. Light often spills from the ventilator slats, and it is worth holding a sheet of black card or a piece of black velvet between the top of the projector and the screen.

● **Choose your screen** with care. A wall painted plain matt white is quite satisfactory, but a proper screen is better.

● **Beaded screens** give a very bright, clear image, but can only be seen over a very narrow angle.

● **Position the screen** facing away from any potential light leaks – that is, up against the window rather than facing it.

● **Set up the projector** level with the middle of the screen.

● **Raise the projector** to the right height on a purpose-built stand. If you improvise, make sure the stand is rigid. A pair of step ladders makes a good base; a pile of telephone directories on the edge of a table does not.

● **Project** through a serving hatch if you can. This will keep a noisy projector out of ear shot. You can change the slides with a remote control switch if you have one.

● **Do not tilt the projector** to gain height. This will distort the image – the top will be bigger than the bottom, an effect called 'keystoning'.

● **Choose the focal length** of your enlarger to suit the size of room you have and the size of image you want. Bear in mind that you need a very powerful projector to project large images well.

● **Keep a spare bulb handy** – bulbs can blow at the most awkward times.

● **Carefully align** all the slides to be shown so that they can be slotted quickly into the projector or the magazine the right way round. Remember, slides are projected upside down with the emulsion facing the screen.

● **Stick spots** on the bottom left-hand corner of your slides to help you with alignment. These go at the top right-hand corner when you feed the slides into the projector.

● **Do not mix** dense and thin slides or different types of film.

# Make a Slide Show

Casually projecting a loosely organized collection of holiday pictures is simple and straightforward. But you may want to attempt something more structured. You may even want to provide an informative commentary, rather than off-the-cuff remarks. Whatever your motive, you will find the results of organizing your slides into a proper show rewarding. By editing and trimming the sequence of images, you will find that their effect is far more concise and powerful. The weak pictures that often dilute the effect of a slide session should be discarded ruthlessly, and the better pictures should be used only if they contribute to the overall effect. You may find this leaves you with very few slides, but this is not such a bad thing.

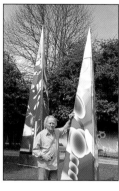

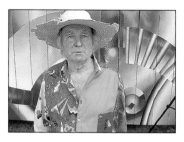

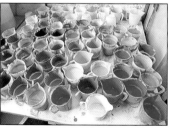

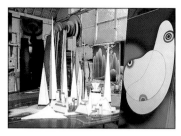

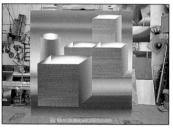

▲ I shot this sequence of slides to illustrate an outdoor art exhibition of the work of Stefan Knapp. To make the slide show more visually appealing I looked for a variety of shots. As well as images of the paintings themselves, I took portraits of the artist himself, and shots of the work in progress in his studio. Useful cutaway shots, such as the paint pots, were also taken to help move from subject to subject without causing a jump on screen – a useful trick used by film-makers. Also to provide variety, I used an assortment of close-ups and wide shots - which not only made for an more interesting show, but also provided the viewers with a scale of reference as to the size of the works. Note that in this case 'close-up' and 'wide' do not refer to the type of lens used but to how much information is included in the picture.

● **Use perfect slides.** Reject any that are blurred, poorly exposed or in any way substandard.

● **Try to keep** the same format – vertical or horizontal. If you need to switch, look for an image with a strong rectangular shape to make the transition. A doorway is ideal.

● **Keep movement** in the slides, such as cars, in the same direction.

● **Make a narrative** to structure the show, running from beginning to end.

● **Aim for variety** of scale and subject. Mix long shots with close-ups and people with places.

● **Look for scene-setting shots,** eg, overall views to introduce a sequence.

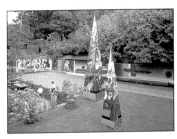

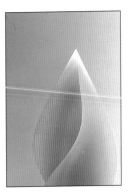

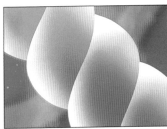

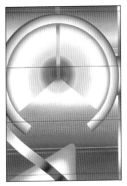

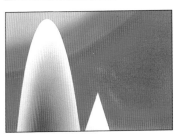

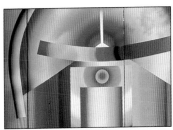

# Exposure Compensation

Printing exposure varies not only between individual negatives, but also for the same negative when you alter the enlarging lens aperture, the magnification or the filtration. However, there is no need to make a new test strip for each change. Simply consult the tables below.

### Changes in print size

| Magnification | Original exposure time (seconds) | | | | | | |
|---|---|---|---|---|---|---|---|
| | 1 | 2 | 4 | 8 | 16 | 20 | 30 |
| | New exposure time (seconds) | | | | | | |
| 2x | 2 | 5½ | 11 | 22 | 44 | 55 | 80 |
| 2.25x | 2½ | 6½ | 13 | 26 | 55 | 65 | 95 |
| 2.5x | 3 | 8 | 16 | 32 | 65 | 80 | 120 |
| 2.75x | 3½ | 9½ | 18 | 37 | 75 | 95 | 140 |
| 3x | 4 | 11 | 22 | 45 | 90 | 110 | 165 |
| 3.5x | 5¼ | 15 | 30 | 60 | 120 | 150 | 220 |
| 4x | 7 | 18 | 38 | 76 | 150 | 200 | 280 |
| 5x | 11 | 30 | 60 | 120 | 240 | 300 | 450 |
| 6x | 16 | 45 | 90 | 180 | 360 | 450 | – |
| 8x | 30 | 80 | 160 | 320 | – | – | – |
| 10x | 50 | 130 | 270 | – | – | – | – |

To find the extra exposure needed for a larger print from a negative, you must work out how many times bigger the new print will be than your original reference print. To do this, simply measure the length of one side in both the original print and the new print. Divide one into the other to find the magnification. Then consult the table above for the new exposure time.

The blank spaces in the table indicate that the new exposure would be so long that 'reciprocity failure' may become a severe problem. It is better not to make giant enlargements from negatives so dense, but if you must, open the aperture to keep the exposure as short as possible and make a test strip. With colour, you may need to alter the filtration.

### Changes in filtration

| Filter strength | Filter factors | | | | | |
|---|---|---|---|---|---|---|
| | Yellow | | Magenta | | Cyan | |
| | Kodak | Agfa | Kodak | Agfa | Kodak | Agfa |
| 05 | 1.1 | 1.1 | 1.2 | 1.2 | 1.1 | 1.2 |
| 10 | 1.1 | 1.1 | 1.3 | 1.2 | 1.2 | 1.2 |
| 20 | 1.1 | 1.2 | 1.5 | 1.2 | 1.3 | 1.3 |
| 30 | 1.1 | 1.2 | 1.7 | 1.3 | 1.4 | 1.4 |
| 40 | 1.1 | 1.2 | 1.9 | 1.4 | 1.5 | 1.5 |
| 50 | 1.1 | 1.2 | 2.1 | 1.5 | 1.6 | 1.7 |

To find the exposure change needed when changing filtration, consult the table to find the filter factor for each new filter added or subtracted. When adding filters, multiply the original exposure by the filter factor to find the new exposure. When subtracting filters, divide by the filter factor. When changing two colours, multiply (or divide) the original exposure time first by the factor for one colour, then by the factor for the other.

## Ilford Multigrade IV Colour filtration settings for grades 0–5

| Enlarger Type* | A | | B | | C | | D | |
|---|---|---|---|---|---|---|---|---|
| Filter Colour | Y | M | Y | M | Y | M | Y | M |
| **Grade** | | | | | | | | |
| 0 | 150 | 25 | 92 | 16 | 75 | 12 | 110 | 60 |
| 0.5 | 110 | 33 | 74 | 22 | 55 | 16 | 73 | 22 |
| 1 | 85 | 42 | 56 | 28 | 42 | 21 | 57 | 28 |
| 1.5 | 70 | 55 | 46 | 37 | 35 | 27 | 46 | 36 |
| 2 | 55 | 70 | 36 | 46 | 37 | 35 | 36 | 46 |
| 2.5 | 42 | 80 | 28 | 53 | 21 | 40 | 28 | 53 |
| 3 | 30 | 90 | 26 | 60 | 15 | 45 | 20 | 60 |
| 3.5 | 18 | 112 | 12 | 75 | 9 | 56 | 12 | 74 |
| 4 | 6 | 135 | 4 | 90 | 3 | 67 | 4 | 90 |
| 4.5 | 0 | 195 | 0 | 130 | 0 | 97 | 0 | 130 |
| 5 | 0 | 200+ | 0 | 130+ | 0 | 97+ | 0 | 130+ |

*Key to enlargers
A – Beseler Chromega, De Vere, Dunco, Jobo, Kaiser, Kodak, LPL, Omega, Paterson, Simmard; B – Durst; C – Meopta; D – Leitz.

---

## Conversion factors

### Length
| | | | | | |
|---|---|---|---|---|---|
| inches to centimetres | x | 2.54 | centimetres to inches | x | 0.3937 |
| feet to metres | x | 0.3048 | metres to feet | x | 3.2808 |

### Volume
| | | | | | |
|---|---|---|---|---|---|
| US fluid ounces to millilitres | x | 29.57 | millilitres to US fluid ounces | x | 0.0338 |
| UK fluid ounces to millilitres | x | 28.41 | millilitres to UK fluid ounces | x | 0.0352 |

### Weight
| | | | | | |
|---|---|---|---|---|---|
| ounces to grams | x | 28.35 | grams to ounces | x | 0.0353 |
| pounds to kilograms | x | 0.4536 | kilograms to pounds | x | 2.2047 |

### Fahrenheit to Centigrade:
degrees C = (degrees F − 32) x 5÷9

### Centigrade to Fahrenheit:
degrees F = (degrees C x 9÷5) + 32

| °F | °C | °F | °C | °C | °F | °C | °F |
|---|---|---|---|---|---|---|---|
| 50 | 10.0 | 75 | 23.89 | 10 | 50.0 | 30 | 86.0 |
| 55 | 12.78 | 80 | 26.67 | 15 | 59.0 | 32 | 89.6 |
| 60 | 15.56 | 85 | 29.44 | 19 | 66.2 | 34 | 93.2 |
| 65 | 18.33 | 90 | 32.22 | 20 | 68.0 | 36 | 96.8 |
| 67 | 19.44 | 95 | 35.00 | 21 | 69.9 | 37 | 98.6 |
| 68 | 20.00 | 100 | 37.78 | 24 | 75.2 | 38 | 100.4 |
| 69 | 20.55 | 101 | 38.34 | 26 | 78.8 | 39 | 102.2 |
| 70 | 21.11 | 105 | 40.56 | 28 | 82.4 | 40 | 104.0 |

# Faults in Film Processing

Defects that can appear in all types of films are listed under the heading 'black-and-white' . Faults specific to colour negative or transparency films are listed under the appropriate headings. Unless otherwise stated, faults in processed film cannot be rectified, and the remedies described refer to future processing technique.

### Black-and-white film

● **Scratches along film length**
Cause: Grit dragged in contact with film, when it is being either wound out of or rewound into film spool, grit dragged along film when it is being passed through fingers or squeegeed prior to drying; possible rough spot on film pressure plate in camera (rare).
Remedy: Protect film reels from dust, grit and sand – do not unwrap film or open package until you are ready to load the film into the camera. With reloadable cassettes, check that felt light trap is clean.Make sure the squeegee is clean before using and/or use lighter pressure.

● **Isolated light or clear areas on negatives**
Cause: Air bubbles have stuck to film during processing.
Remedy: Tap the developing tank after agitation to dislodge air bubbles.

● **Dark streaks and/or blobs of irregular shape**
Cause: A light leak has locally fogged the film before it was developed.
Remedy: prevent by checking reusable film cassettes and light-tightness of darkroom and developing tank. Ensure that a gasket is used between the developing tank and its lid and that the tank has no hairline cracks.

● **Clear or light band along edge of film**
Cause: Insufficient solution in developing tank to completely cover the film.
Remedy: Follow the tank directions to ensure that enough solution is used for the quantity and format of films being processed (check using clear water).

● **Negatives too dense and contrast too high**
Cause: The development temperature was too high, or the developing time too long, or the agitation during development was excessive.
Remedy: Farmer's reducer can make thick negatives somewhat thinner. In future, check the developer directions for the correct time, temperature and agitation for the particular film being processed, and control the temperature of the solution by placing it in a water bath constantly adjusted to the correct temperature. If this is impossible, adjust the developing time to the temperature actually used.

● **Negatives too thin but contrast near normal**
Cause: The development temperature was too low, or the development time too short, or the agitation during development was insufficient.
Remedy: Control the development process as described as above.

● **Milky white appearance**
Cause: Insufficient fixing bath time, exhausted fixer or incorrect fixer concentration.
Remedy: Try refixing in new solution, check manufacturers' recommendations concerning dilution and the amount of use. Mark your reusable fixer solution bottle with date of mixing, concentration and the number of films that one batch will treat.

● **Overall crazed pattern ('reticulation')**
Cause: The 'shock' of inconsistent solution temperatures – for example, warm developer and cold fixer.
Remedy: Make sure that all solutions and the water wash are kept at the same temperature.

● **Film completely clear**
Cause: Film accidentally placed in fixer instead of developer.
Remedy: None for affected films.

### Colour negative film

● **Negatives too dense and contrasty**
Cause: Overdevelopment; on Agfa film, if the orange mask is also too dense, then the likely cause is excessive bleaching.
Remedy: Follow the manufacturer's directions on time and temperature. Avoid excessive tank draining times.

● **Negatives too contrasty, density normal**
Cause: Excessive bleaching.
Remedy: Check maker's directions regarding bleaching time, temperature and dilution.

● **Spots** in which the orange mask can be seen but no image, or only a faint one
Cause: Air bubbles stuck to film during processing.
Remedy: Tap the tank after agitation.

● **Irregularly shaped streaks**
running downwards from the film's sprocket holes
Cause: Developer was caught in holes during excessive draining time.
Remedy: Start to drain slightly before that stage is completed, and progress quickly to the next stage.

● **Purple cast** with a dense image
Cause: Fogging.
Remedy: Check the light-tightness of the developing tank and of the darkroom itself.

### Colour slide film

● **Light-coloured streaks** or irregular spots, often yellowish
Cause: Fogging.
Remedy: Check the light-tightness of the developing tank and the darkroom.

● **Dark spots,** possibly with a reddish cast
Cause: Air bubbles sticking to the film during development.

Remedy: After agitation, tap the tank bottom sharply.

● **Film too dense and dark, with a reddish cast**
Cause: Underdevelopment
Remedy: Use fresh chemicals. Mark the quantity for which a batch can be used on the bottle. Check the directions for proper time, temperature and dilution.

● **Too blue, with smoky blacks**
Cause: Reversal bath (if the film was chemically reversed) was too concentrated; the colour developer was too weak; or the first developer was contaminated.
Remedy: Carefully label bottles and always use the same bottles for the same solutions. Check the directions for the correct dilutions.

● **Green cast, with smoky blacks**
Cause: Reversal procedure was omitted or inadequate, or film was outdated or badly stored.
Remedy: Check that fresh solutions are being used. Check time, temperature and agitation for the reversal procedure (if chemical), or check lamp wattage and film-to-lamp distance against the directions.

● **Too light, with a blue cast**
Cause: Colour developer possibly contaminated with first developer.
Remedy: Label bottles correctly and always use the same bottles for the same solutions.

● **Milky, cloudy appearance**
Cause: Inadequate fixing time, incorrect fixer concentration, fixer exhausted or too cold.
Remedy: Refix in fresh solution.

● **Highlight areas appear pink**
Cause: Insufficient wash following the colour development stage.
Remedy: Follow directions.

● **Yellow-brown staining**
Cause: Inadequate bleaching procedure.
Remedy: Rebleach and repeat fixing, washing and drying stages.

# Faults in Printing

Faults common to all types of printing are listed with those relating to black and white printing; those specific to colour printing are listed under the appropriate headings. Apart from minor blemishes that can be retouched, faults in prints cannot be corrected, and the remedies described here can be applied only in subsequent printing.

### Black-and-white printing

● **Low contrast, with poor black-and-white tones**
Cause: Underdevelopment, the paper is fogged.
Remedy: Try a higher grade of paper. Check the agitation time, temperature and dilution directions of the developer. Guard against fogging the paper – do not expose it to the safelight for too long before processing, or place it too close to the safelight. Ensure that the safelight is not too strong and is of the right type, and do not leave the lid of the paper box off while making a print.

● **High contrast** with compressed range of greys
Cause: Overdevelopment.
Remedy: Check the developer directions concerning agitation, time and temperature.

● **Image too dark**
Cause: Overexposure in printing; overdevelopment; paper fogged.
Remedy: Make a second test strip to confirm the exposure time. Check that the lens was stopped down to the correct aperture. Check the developer directions for the recommended time, temperature, agitation and dilution. Check that the paper stock has not been fogged – check the paper's box, the safelight directions and the darkroom's light-tightness.

● **White spots**
Cause: Air bubbles on the print during development.
Remedy: Agitate the print constantly while it is in the developer.

● **White branched, lightning-like marks**
Cause: Static electricity has marked the print or negative slightly.
Remedy: If the marks are on the negative, retouch the print.

● **Blue, purple or brownish stains**
Cause: Developer contaminated from fixer or stop bath.
Remedy: Remix chemicals. Avoid carry-over.

● **Dark streaks**
Cause: Excessive draining time after development; or fixer solution is too weak.
Remedy: Drain print quickly after development. Use fresh fixer solution.

● **Uneven, patchy image**
Cause: Insufficient solution level in tray, or the print was taken from the developer before fully developed, in an attempt to compensate for overexposure.
Remedy: Use more solution in each tray and check that the print is always covered by the solutions. Give all prints full development time.

● **Blotchy image with yellowish-white tones**
Cause: Old or incorrectly stored paper stock.
Remedy: Store paper on its side in a cool, dry, dark place and use it as soon as possible.

● **Light rings on the image**
Cause: Interference rings ('Newton's rings') caused by a poor fit between negative and carrier glass.
Remedy: Use a specially designed glass or use a glassless negative carrier.

### Printing from colour negatives

● **Overall colour cast**
Cause: Wrong filtration.

Remedy: Add a combination of filters which correspond to the colour of the cast, or remove a combination with the complementary colour.

● **Cyan stains**
Cause: Partial contamination of developer.
Remedy: Remix developer. Avoid carry-over.

● **Reddish, magenta or pink stain overall**
Cause: Oxidized developer; improper storage; old solutions; insufficient wash time.
Remedy: Use fresh developer. Store solutions correctly and check the mixing date.

● **Cyan or blue streaks**
Cause: Developer contaminating bleach/fix.
Remedy: Thoroughly drain the print tube after the developer stage. Use clean beakers.

● **Light patchy areas**
Cause: Paper curled the wrong way when loaded into the print drum.
Remedy: Load the paper with its emulsion inwards.

### Printing from slides

**ILFOCHROME A PROCESS**
● **Colour cast**
Cause: Incorrect filtration.
Remedy: Subtract a filter combination of the same colour, or add the complementary colour.

● **Light image with greenish highlights,** and dull black shadow areas
Cause: Development time too long.
Remedy: Check processing time with directions. Check test print.

● **Foggy, dull print**
Cause: Insufficient bleach time; or bleach too weak or exhausted.
Remedy: Check bleach time and dilution. Use fresh bleach if necessary.

● **Dull and dark print**
Cause: Contaminated bleach/fix solution.
Remedy: Remix and avoid carry-over.

● **Low contrast cast**
Cause: Fixer omitted, exhausted or too weak.
Remedy: Check the dilution of the fixer. Check that the fixing step was not omitted.

● **Black print with no image**
Cause: Bleach bath omitted.
Remedy: Always use beakers and bottles in the same order to avoid missing out a step.

● **Light image with overall blue cast**
Cause: Developer solution too concentrated.
Remedy: Check the dilution against the manufacturers' instructions.

**EKTACHROME R3000 PROCESS**
● **Cyan cast overall**
Cause: First developer contaminated with bleach/fixer.
Remedy: Remix fresh developer; avoid carry-over. Use clean chemical beakers.

● **Blue or reddish cast overall**
Cause: Insufficient first or second wash respectively.
Remedy: Increase the appropriate wash time, temperature and/or flow of water.

● **Magenta cast on a dark print**
Cause: Insufficient colour development.
Remedy: Check the directions for correct time, temperature, dilution and agitation.

● **Blue cast in shadow areas**
Cause: Insufficient colour development.
Remedy: Check the directions for correct time, temperature, dilution and agitation.

● **Foggy, low-contrast highlights**
Cause: Insufficient bleach/fix procedure, contaminated first developer.
Remedy: Check directions. Mix fresh developing solution.

# Glossary

Words shown in capitals indicate cross references within the glossary.

## A

**Aberration.** Inherent fault in a lens image. Aberrations include ASTIGMATISM, BARREL DISTORTION, CHROMATIC ABERRATION, COMA, SPHERICAL ABERRATION. COMPOUND LENSES minimize aberrations.

**Accelerator.** Alkali in a DEVELOPER, used to speed up its action.

**Actinic.** Describes light which is able to affect photographic material. With ordinary film, visible light and some ultraviolet light is actinic, while infrared light is not.

**Acutance.** Objective measure of image sharpness.

**Additive colour printing.** A method of filtration occasionally used in making prints from colour negatives. Three successive EXPOSURES of the negative are made, with red, green and blue light respectively. See also SUBTRACTIVE COLOUR PRINTING.

**Air bells.** Bubbles of air clinging to the emulsion surface during processing, which prevent uniform chemical action. Prevented by agitation.

**Airbrush.** An instrument used by photographers for retouching prints. It uses a controlled flow of compressed air to spray paint or dye.

**Anamorphic lens.** Special type of lens that compresses the image in one dimension by means of cylindrical or prismatic elements. The image can be restored to normal by using a similar lens for printing or projection.

**Angle of view.** Strictly the angle subtended by the diagonal of the film format at the rear NODAL POINT of the lens. Generally taken to mean the wider angle 'seen' by a given lens. The longer the focal length of a lens, the narrower its angle of view. See also COVERING POWER.

**Aperture.** Strictly, the opening that limits the amount of light reaching the film and hence the brightness of the image. In some cameras the aperture is of a fixed size; in others it is in the form of an opening in a barrier called the DIAPHRAGM and can be varied in size. (An iris diaphragm forms a continuously variable opening, while a stop plate has a number of holes of varying sizes.) Photographers, however, generally use the term 'aperture' to refer to the size of this opening. See also F NUMBER.

**ASA.** American Standards Association, which devised one of the two early systems for rating the SPEED of an emulsion. See also DIN and ISO.

**Astigmatism.** The inability of a lens to focus vertical and horizontal lines in the same FOCAL PLANE. Corrected lenses are called 'anastigmatic'.

## B

**Back projection.** Projection of slides onto a translucent screen from behind, instead of onto the front of a reflective screen.

**Barrel distortion.** Lens defect characterized by the distortion of straight lines at the edges of an image so that they curve inward at the corners of the frame.

**Bas relief.** In photography the name given to the special effect created when a negative and positive are sandwiched together and printed slightly out of register. The resulting picture gives the impression of being carved in low relief, like a bas-relief sculpture.

**Beaded screen.** Type of front-projection screen. The surface is covered with minute glass beads, giving a brighter picture than a plain white screen.

**Bellows.** Light-tight folding bag made of pleated material used to join the lens to the camera body. Found on large studio cameras, and used as an accessory for close-up work with smaller formats.

**Between-the-lens shutter.** One of two main types of shutter. Situated close to the diaphragm, it consists of thin metal blades or leaves that spring open and then close when the camera is fired, exposing the film. See also FOCAL-PLANE SHUTTER.

**Bleaching.** Chemical process for removing black metallic silver from the emulsion by converting it to a compound that may be dissolved.

**Bleach out process.** Technique of producing a line drawing based on a photographic image. The outlines of a photograph are drawn over with pencil or waterproof ink, then the silver image is bleached away, leaving only the outline behind.

**Bracketing.** Technique for ensuring the correct EXPOSURE by taking several photographs of the same subject at slightly different exposure settings. The bracketed sequence is usually taken with exposures at regular STOP intervals.

**Bromide paper.** Photographic paper for printing enlargements. The basic light-sensitive ingredient in the emulsion is silver bromide.

**B setting.** The setting on the shutter speed dial of a camera at which the SHUTTER remains open for as long as the release button is held down, allowing longer EXPOSUREs than the preset speeds on the camera. The 'B' stands for 'bulb' for historical reasons. See also T SETTING.

**BSI.** British Standards Institution, which has an independent system of rating emulsion speed, similar to the ASA system. However, the BSI system is used industrially.

**Bulk loader.** Device for handling film that has been bought in bulk in a single length and which needs to be cut and loaded into cassettes.

**Burning in.** Technique used in printing when a small area of the print requires more EXPOSURE than the rest. After normal exposure, the main area is shielded with a card or by the hands while the detail (such as a highlight that is too dense on the negative) receives further exposure. See also DODGING.

## C

**Callier effect.** Phenomenon that accounts for the higher contrast produced by enlargers using a condenser system, compared to those using a diffuser system. This effect, first investigated by André Callier in 1909, is explained by the fact that the light focused by the condenser onto the lens of the enlarger is partly scattered by the negative before it reaches the lens. The denser parts of the negative scatter the most light and therefore the contrast is increased. In a diffuser enlarger, on the other hand, all areas of the negative cause the same amount of scattering.

**Calotype.** Print made by an early photographic process from paper negatives. Iodized paper requiring lengthy EXPOSURE was used in the camera. The system was patented by Fox Talbot in 1841, but became obsolete with the introduction of the COLLODION PROCESS. Also known as a Talbotype.

**Canada balsam.** Resin used to cement together pieces of optical glass, such as elements of a lens. When set it has a refractive index almost exactly equal to that of glass. It is obtained from the balsam fir of North America.

**Cartridge.** Plastic container of film such as the old 126 or 110 formats. The film is wound inside the cartridge from one spool onto a second spool.

**Cassette.** Container for 35mm or APS film. After EXPOSURE the film is wound back onto the cassette spool before the camera is opened.

**Cast.** Overall shift towards a particular hue, giving colour photographs an unnatural appearance.

**CdS cell.** Photosensitive cell used in some light meters, incorporating a cadmium sulphide resistor, which regulates electric current.

**Centre-weighted meter.** Type of through-the-lens light meter. The reading is most strongly influenced by the intensity of light at the center of the image.

**Chlorobromide papers.** Printing papers coated with a compound of silver bromide and silver chloride, giving warm tones.

**Chromatic aberration.** The inability of a lens to focus different colours on the same focal plane.

**Chromogenic.** Chromogenic means literally 'colour forming', and chromogenic films and papers are materials in which the final image is made of coloured dyes formed during processing rather than silver.

**Chromopathic.** See DYE DESTRUCTION PROCESS.

**Circle of confusion.** A disc of light on the image produced by a lens when a point on the subject is not perfectly brought into focus. When looking at a photograph, the eye cannot distinguish between an extremely small circle of confusion (with a diameter of less than 0.25mm – a hundredth of an inch) and a true point.

**Cold cathode enlarger.** Type of enlarger using as its light source a special fluorescent tube with a low working temperature. Particularly suitable for large-format work.

**Collodion process.** Wet-plate photographic process introduced in 1851 by F. Scott Archer, remaining in use until the 1880s. It superseded DAGUERREOTYPE and CALOTYPE.

**Colour analyser.** Electronic device that assesses the correct filtration for a colour print.

**Colour conversion filters.** Camera filters required when daylight colour film is used in artificial light, or when film balanced for artificial light is used in daylight.

**Colour correction filters.** Filters used to correct slight irregularities in colour caused by specific light sources. Also refers to the cyan, magenta and yellow filters that are used to balance the colour of prints made from colour negatives.

**Colour negative film.** Film giving colour negatives, intended for printing.

**Colour reversal film.** Film giving colour positives (called slides or transparencies). Prints can also be made directly from these positives using special paper and chemicals.

**Colour temperature.** Measure of the relative blueness or redness of a light source, expressed in KELVIN. The human eye adjusts to differences in colour temperature automatically most of the time, but colour film is balanced to work with a single colour temperature – usually average daylight, or tungsten bulb lighting.

**Coma.** A lens defect that results in off-axis points of light appearing in the image not as points but as discs with comet-like tails.

**Combination printing.** General term for techniques in which more than one negative is printed onto a single sheet of paper.

**Compound lens.** Lens consisting of more than one element, designed so that the faults of the various elements largely cancel each other out.

**Condenser.** Optical system consisting of one or two plano-convex lenses (flat on one side, curving outward on the other) used in an enlarger or slide projector to concentrate light from a source and focus it on the negative or slide.

**Contact print.** Print that is the same size as the negative, made by sandwiching together the negative and the photographic paper when making the print. A whole roll of 35mm film can be contact printed at once onto one sheet of 10 x 8in (25.4 x 20.3cm) paper.

**Converging lens.** Any lens that is thicker in the middle than at the edges. Such lenses are able to cause parallel light to converge onto a point of focus, giving an image. Also known as a positive lens.

**Converging verticals.** Distorted appearance of vertical lines in an image, produced when the camera is tilted upwards. Tall objects such as buildings, for instance, appear to be leaning backward. Can be partially corrected at the printing stage, or by the use of camera movements.

**Converter.** Auxiliary lens, usually fitted between the camera body and the principal lens, giving a combined FOCAL LENGTH that is greater than that of the principal lens alone. Most converters increase focal length by a factor of two or three. Also known as teleconverters.

**Convertible lens.** Compound lens consisting of two lens assemblies used separately or together. The two sections are usually of differing focal lengths, giving three possible permutations.

**Correction filters.** Colour filters used over the camera lens to modify the tonal balance of black-and-white images. See COLOUR CORRECTION FILTERS.

**Covering power.** The largest image area of acceptable quality that a given lens produces. The covering power of a lens is usually only slightly greater than the standard negative size for which it is intended. However, in a lens designed for use with a camera with movements, the covering power must be considerably greater.

**Cropping.** Enlarging only a selected portion of the negative instead of printing the entire area.

# D

**Daguerreotype.** Early photographic picture made on a copper plate coated with polished silver and sensitized with silver iodide. The image was developed using mercury vapour, giving a direct positive. The process was introduced by Louis Daguerre in 1839, and was the first to be commercially successful.

**Daylight film.** Colour film balanced to give accurate colour rendering in average daylight, that is to say, when the COLOUR TEMPERATURE of the light source is around 5500° Kelvin. Also suitable for use with electronic flash.

**Density.** The light-absorbing power of a photographic image. A logarithmic scale is used in measurements: 50% absorption is expressed as 0.3, 100% is expressed as 1.0, etc. In general terms, density is simply the opaqueness of a negative or the blackness of a print.

**Depth of field.** Zone of acceptable sharpness extending in front of and behind the plane of the subject that is exactly focused by the lens.

**Depth of focus.** Very narrow zone behind the lens within which slight variation in the position of the film makes no appreciable difference to the focusing of the image.

**Developer.** Chemical agent that converts the LATENT IMAGE into a visible image.

**Developer improvers.** Chemicals with anti-fog properties that can be added to developing solutions or may already be included in the ingredients of a developer (see FOG).

**Diaphragm.** System of adjustable metal blades forming a roughly circular opening of variable diameter, used to control the APERTURE of a lens.

**Diapositive.** Alternative name for TRANSPARENCY.

**Dichroic fog.** Processing fault characterized by a stain of reddish and greenish colours. Caused by the use of exhausted FIXER whose acidity is insufficient to halt the development entirely. A fine deposit of silver is formed that appears reddish by transmitted light and greenish by reflected light.

**Differential focusing.** Technique involving the use of shallow depth of field to enhance the illusion of depth and solidity in a photograph.

**Diffraction.** Phenomenon occurring when light passes close to the edge of an opaque body or through a narrow APERTURE. The light is slightly deflected, setting up interference patterns that may sometimes be seen by the naked eye as fuzziness. The effect is occasionally noticeable in photography, when, for example, a very small lens aperture is used.

**DIN.** Deutsche Industrie Norm, the German standards association that devised one of the old systems used for rating the speed of an EMULSION. On the DIN scale, every increase of 3 indicates that the sensitivity of the emulsion has doubled. See ASA and ISO.

**Diverging lens.** Any lens that is thicker at the edges than in the middle. Such lenses cause parallel rays of light to diverge, forming an image on the same side of the lens as the subject. Diverging lenses are also known as NEGATIVE LENSES.

**D-max.** Technical term for the maximum DENSITY of which a given EMULSION is capable.

**Dodging.** Technique used in printing photographs when one area of the print is given less EXPOSURE than the rest. A hand or a piece of card is used to prevent the selected area from receiving the full exposure. The 'dodged' areas thus remain darker. See also BURNING IN.

**Drift-by technique.** Processing technique used to allow for the cooling of a chemical bath (in most cases, the developer) during the time it is in contact with the EMULSION. Before use, the solution is warmed to a point slightly above the required temperature, so that while it is being used it cools to a temperature slightly below, but still within the margin of safety.

**Drying marks.** Blemishes on the EMULSION resulting from uneven drying. Also residue left on the film after water from the wash has evaporated.

**Dry mounting.** Method of mounting prints onto card using a special heat-sensitive adhesive tissue.

**Dye coupler.** Chemical responsible for producing the appropriate coloured dyes during the development of a colour photograph. Dye couplers may be incorporated in the EMULSION, or they may be part of the DEVELOPER.

**Dye destruction process.** System for forming colour images by selectively eliminating dyes during processing. it makes use of a tripack material in which the three dyes are ready-formed before exposure. After exposure, a bleaching agent is used to destroy the dyes in proportion to the development of the silver halide image. Dyes are therefore destroyed most in exposed areas. This means it is possible to produce positive prints from colour transparencies without reversal.

# E

**Edge effects.** Development phenomena characterized by increased contrast at the boundaries of areas with markedly different densities. The effects are produced when developer becomes rapidly exhausted in heavily exposed areas, and fresher developer from the adjacent area moves across to replace it. Thus the edge of the heavily exposed area receives more development than the average for that area (the displaced fresh developer penetrating only slightly into the area), and the edge of the adjacent, lightly exposed area receives less development than the average for that area, some of its development potential having been lost to the edge of the heavily exposed area. The resulting increased sharpness is an effect called ACUTANCE that is sometimes sought after, and can be emphasized by using a developer that exhausts rapidly and by avoiding agitation.

**Electronic flash.** Type of flash-gun that uses the flash of light produced by a high-voltage electrical discharge between two electrodes in a gas-filled tube.

**Emulsion.** In photography, the light-sensitive layer of a photographic material. The emulsion consists essentially of SILVER HALIDE crystals suspended in GELATIN.

**Enlargement.** Photographic print larger than the original image on the film.

**Exposure.** Total amount of light allowed to reach the light-sensitive material during the formation of the LATENT IMAGE. The exposure is dependent on the brightness of the image, the camera APERTURE, and on the length of time for which the photographic material is exposed.

**Exposure meter.** Instrument for measuring the intensity of light so as to determine the correct SHUTTER and APERTURE settings.

**Extension tubes.** Accessories used in close-up photography, consisting of metal tubes that can be fitted between the lens and camera body, thus increasing the lens-to-film distance.

## F

**Farmer's reducer.** Solution of potassium ferricyanide and sodium thiosulphate, used in photography to bleach negatives and prints. See REDUCER.

**Fast lens.** Lens with a wide maximum APERTURE, relative to its FOCAL LENGTH.

**Film speed.** The film's sensitivity to light, expressed as a rating on the ISO scale.

**Filter.** Transparent sheet usually made of glass or plastic that is used to block a specific part of the light passing through it or to change or distort the image in some way. See also COLOUR CONVERSION FILTERS, COLOUR CORRECTION FILTERS, CORRECTION FILTERS and POLARIZING FILTERS.

**Filter pack.** Assembly of filters used in an enlarger when making colour prints. Normally consists of any two of the three subtractive primaries (yellow, magenta, cyan) in the appropriate strengths.

**Fisheye lens.** Extreme wide-angle lens, with an ANGLE OF VIEW of about 180°.

**Fixed-focus lens.** Lens permanently focused at a fixed distance, usually the HYPERFOCAL DISTANCE. Most cheap cameras use this system, giving sharp pictures from about 2 m (6 ft) to INFINITY.

**Fixer.** Chemical bath needed to fix the photographic image permanently after it has been developed. The fixer stabilizes the EMULSION by converting the undeveloped SILVER HALIDES into water-soluble compounds, which can then be dissolved away.

**Flare.** Unwanted light reflected inside the camera or between the elements of the lens giving rise to irregular marks on the negative and degrading the quality of the image. This can be overcome to some extent by using a lens coating, or a LENS HOOD.

**Flashbulb.** Expendable bulb with a filament of metal foil which is designed to burn up very rapidly giving a brief, intense flare of light, sufficiently bright to allow a photograph to be taken. Most flashbulbs have a light blue plastic coating, which gives the flash a COLOUR TEMPERATURE close to that of daylight.

**Flashing.** Technique involving deliberately fogging a print briefly with white light during exposure. The effect is to control contrast. The extra exposure may be spread equally over the whole print, producing a soft overall effect; it may be used for vignetting so that the image merges into a black border, or it may be directed to a particular area by means of a torch to cause local darkening.

**F number.** Aperture setting. The number refers to the focal length of the lens divided by the diameter of the APERTURE. Because F numbers are reciprocals, the bigger the number the smaller the aperture – thus f32 is smaller than f8. The f numbers available with a particular lens and camera generally follow a standard sequence, in which the interval between one STOP and the next represents a halving or doubling in the image brightness.

**Focal length.** The distance between the optical centre of the lens and the point at which rays of light parallel to the optical axis are brought to a focus. In general, the greater the focal length of a lens, the smaller its ANGLE OF VIEW.

**Focal plane.** Plane on which a given subject is brought to a sharp focus, which is the same as the plane on which the film is positioned.

**Focal-plane shutter.** One of the main types of SHUTTER, used almost universally in SINGLE-LENS REFLEX cameras. Positioned behind the lens (but slightly in front of the FOCAL PLANE), the shutter consists of a system of blinds or blades. When the camera is fired, a slit travels across the image area either vertically or horizontally. The width and the speed of travel of the slit determine the duration of the EXPOSURE. See also BETWEEN-THE-LENS SHUTTER.

**Fog.** Veiling of an image caused by accidentally exposing the film or paper; by overactive developer or weak fixer containing heavy deposits of silver salts; by overlong storage; or by exposure to powerful X-rays. See also DEVELOPER IMPROVERS.

**Forced development.** Technique used to increase the effective speed of a film by extending its normal development time. Also known as 'PUSHING' the film.

**Format.** Dimensions of the image recorded on the film by a given type of camera.

**Fresnel lens.** A lens whose surface consists of a series of concentric circular 'steps', each of which is shaped like part of the surface of a convex lens. Fresnel lenses are often used in the focusing screens of cameras to help improve the brightness of the image seen through the viewfinder. They are also used in spotlights to concentrate the light beam.

## G

**Gelatin.** Material used as a binding for the EMULSION of photographic paper and film.

**Glazing.** Process by which glossy prints can be given a shiny finish by being dried in contact with a hot drum or plate of chromium or steel.

**Grain.** Granular texture that appears to a degree in all processed photographic materials. In black-and-white photographs the grains are clumps of particles of black metallic silver that constitute the dark areas of a photograph. In colour photographs the silver has been removed chemically but tiny blotches of dye retain the appearance of graininess. The faster the film the coarser the texture of the grain.

**Granularity.** Measure of graininess.

**Guide number.** Number indicating the effective power of a flash unit. For a given FILM SPEED, the guide number divided by the distance between the flash and the subject gives the appropriate F NUMBER to use.

## H

**Halation.** Phenomenon characterized by a halo-like band around the developed image of a bright light source. It is caused by internal reflection of light from the support of the EMULSION (in other words, the paper of the print or the base layer of a film).

**Half-frame.** Film format that measures 24x18mm, half the size of standard-format 35mm pictures.

**Halogens.** A group of chemical elements, including fluorine, chlorine, bromine and iodine. These elements are important in that they combine with silver to form SILVER HALIDES – the light-sensitive substances found in all photographic materials.

**Hardener.** Chemical used to strengthen the GELATIN of an EMULSION against physical damage.

**High-contrast developers.** Highly alkaline developers using the chemical hydroquinone alone as developing agent. They yield very high contrast results, especially with lith films.

**High-key.** Picture containing predominantly light tones. See also LOW-KEY.

**High-speed processing.** Method of rapid developing and fixing of photographic materials when conventional processing techniques are too slow, for example for daily newspapers. Some people make up their own solution of such developers as Ilford's liquid Autophen, ID11 or Microphen, warmed to just below the point where chemical fog might be a hazard. Negatives can be developed in 20 seconds, fixed in two minutes with a rapid fixer, and dried in two minutes. Monobath developers, which also incorporate a fixing agent, can develop and fix a black-and-white film in three minutes while still in the cassette and in daylight; a disadvantage is a considerable loss of contrast.

**Highlights.** Brightest area of the subject. In the negative these are areas of greatest DENSITY.

**Holography.** Technique whereby information is recorded on a photographic plate as an interference pattern which, when viewed under the appropriate conditions, yields a three-dimensional image. Holography bears little relation to conventional photography except in its use of a light-sensitive film.

**Hot-shoe.** Accessory plate on a camera for holding a flash-gun in position, and incorporating a live contact for firing the flash when the SHUTTER is fired.

**Hue.** The quality that distinguishes between colours of the same saturation and brightness, the quality, for example, of redness or greenness.

**Hypo.** Colloquial name for sodium thiosulphate, which was once used universally as a fixing agent. The term was thus a synonym for FIXER.

# I

**Incident light.** Light falling on the subject. When a subject is being photographed, readings may be taken of the incident light instead of the reflected light.

**Indicator.** Chemicals added to a processing bath to indicate certain features about its effectiveness and condition (particularly the pH factor).

**Infrared radiation.** Part of the spectrum of electromagnetic radiation, having wavelengths longer than visible red light (approximately 700 to 15,000 nanometers). Infrared radiation is felt as heat, and can be recorded on special types of photographic film. See IR SETTING.

**Integral tripack.** Composite photographic emulsion used in virtually all colour films and papers, comprising three layers, each of which is sensitized to one of the three primary colours.

**Intensification.** Technique of increasing the image density of a thin black-and-white negative, either with a chemical or dye intensifier, or by optical means. In the chemical process the negative is immersed in chemical baths that increase the size of the silver halide grains. This increases contrast. Silver areas of the image can also be treated with dye toners, increasing the opacity of the negative and thus partially stopping the lightwaves passing from the enlarger to the print. Optical treatment by IRRADIATION consists of photographing the negative by a raking side light.

**Intermittency effect.** Phenomenon observed when an EMULSION is given a series of brief EXPOSURES. The DENSITY of the image thus produced is lower than the image density produced by a single exposure equal to the total duration of the short exposures.

**Inverse square law.** Rule that states that for a point source of light, the intensity of light decreases with the square of the distance from the source. Thus when the distance is double, the light intensity is reduced by a factor of four.

**IR (infrared) setting.** A mark sometimes found on the focusing ring of a camera indicating the shift in focus needed when using black-and-white infrared film. Infrared radiation is refracted less than visible light, and the infrared image is therefore brought into focus slightly behind the visible one.

**Irradiation.** Internal scattering of light inside photographic emulsions during exposure, caused by reflections from the SILVER HALIDE crystals.

**ISO.** Scale introduced by the International Standards Organization for the measurement of FILM SPEED, which combines the figures previously used in the ASA and DIN scales. The full rating for a medium-speed film is therefore ISO 100/21° – this however is usually abbreviated to ISO 100. The larger the number the faster, and more sensitive, the EMULSION. The scale is arranged so that a film rated at ISO 200 is twice as fast as one rated at ISO 100, while one rated at ISO 400 is four times as fast.

## J

**Joule.** Unit of energy in the SI (Système International) system of units. The joule is used in photography to indicate the output of an electronic flash.

## K

**Kelvin (K).** Unit used to measure COLOUR TEMPERATURE.

## L

**Laser.** Acronym for Light Amplification by Stimulated Emission of Radiation. Device for producing an intense beam of coherent light that is of a single very pure colour. Used in the production of holograms (see HOLOGRAPHY).

**Latensification.** Technique used to increase effective film speed by fogging the film, either chemically or with light, between exposure and development.

**Latent image.** Invisible image recorded on photographic EMULSION after EXPOSURE, but before development by chemicals.

**Latitude.** Tolerance of photographic material to variations in EXPOSURE.

**Lens hood.** Simple lens accessory, usually made of rubber or plastic, used to shield the lens from light coming from areas outside the field of view – thus preventing FLARE.

**Lith film.** Very high contrast film used to eliminate grey tones and reduce the image to areas of pure black or pure white.

**Long-focus lens.** Lens of focal length greater than that of the STANDARD LENS for a given format. Long-focus lenses have a narrow field of view, and consequently make distant objects appear closer. See also TELEPHOTO LENS.

**Low-key.** Picture containing predominantly dark tones. See also HIGH-KEY.

# M

**Mackie line.** A line that can appear around a highlight on a silver halide emulsion. It is produced by the lateral diffusion of exhausted developer that causes EDGE EFFECTS. See also SABATTIER EFFECT.

**Macro lens.** Strictly, a lens capable of giving an image that is life-size or bigger – a magnification ratio of 1:1 or greater. The term is used to describe any close-focusing lens. Macro lenses can also be used at ordinary subject distances.

**Macrophotography.** Close-up photography in the range of magnification between life-size and about ten times life-size.

**Magnification ratio.** Ratio of image size to object size. The magnification ratio is used to judge the capabilities of a MACRO LENS, and can also be useful in calculating the correct EXPOSURE for close-ups.

**Masking.** Term used to describe ways in which light is prevented from reaching selected areas of an image for various purposes. Some enlargers, for example, incorporate masking devices that cut down stray light passing around the negative or transparency. A masking frame is placed beneath the enlarger lens to establish print size, determine proportions of the picture and keep the paper flat.

**Mercury vapour lamp.** Type of light source sometimes used in studio photography, giving a bluish light. The light is produced by passing an electric current through a tube filled with mercury vapour.

**Metol.** Developing agent, available under various brand names. It is a white crystalline powder that may cause an allergic reaction.

**Microphotography.** Technique used to copy documents and similar materials onto a very small-format film, so that a large amount of information may be stored compactly. The term is sometimes also used to refer to the technique of taking photographs through a microscope, otherwise known as PHOTOMICROGRAPHY.

**Microprism.** Special type of focusing screen composed of a grid of tiny prisms, often incorporated into the standard viewing screens of manual-focus SLR cameras. The microprism gives a fragmented image when the image is out of focus.

**Mired.** Acronym for micro-reciprocal degree. Unit on a scale of COLOUR TEMPERATURE used to calibrate COLOUR CORRECTION FILTERS. The mired value of a light is derived by dividing one million by the colour temperature in Kelvin.

**Mirror lens.** TELEPHOTO lens of a compact design whose construction is based on a combination of lenses and curved mirrors. Light rays from the subject are reflected backward and forward inside the barrel of the lens before reaching the film plane. Also known as a catadioptric lens. Because of its compact design, a mirror lens can be used as a telephoto lens that is smaller and lighter than its traditionally constructed equivalent.

**Monobath.** See HIGH-SPEED PROCESSING.

**Montage.** Composite photographic image made from several different original pictures.

**Motor drive.** Battery-powered camera feature or accessory used to wind the film on automatically after each shot, and to rewind the film at the end of the roll. Fast motorwinds can be used to take several pictures a second, when shooting sport, for example.

**MQ/PQ developers.** Popular general purpose developing solutions containing the chemicals metol and hydroquinone or phenidone and hydroquinone.

**Multigrade paper.** See VARIABLE CONTRAST PAPER.

# N

**Negative.** Image in which light tones are recorded as dark tones, and vice versa. In colour negatives every colour in the original subject is represented by its complementary colour.

**Negative lens.** See DIVERGING LENS.

**Neutral density filter.** Uniformly grey filter that reduces the brightness of an image without altering its colour content. Used when the light is too bright for the film being used. A graduated neutral density filter (which is grey at the top and clear at the bottom) is used to reduce contrast in landscape photography between a bright sky and a darker foreground.

**Newton's rings.** Narrow multi-coloured bands that appear when two transparent surfaces are sandwiched together with imperfect contact. The pattern is caused by interference, and can be troublesome when slides or negatives are held between glass or plastic.

**Nodal point.** Point of intersection between the optical axis of a compound lens and one of the two principal planes of refraction. A compound lens thus has a front and a rear nodal point from which its basic measurements (such as FOCAL LENGTH) are made.

**Normal lens.** See STANDARD LENS.

# O

**Opacity.** An objective measurement of the degree of opaqueness of a material; the ratio of incident light to transmitted light.

**Opalescent sheet.** A sheet of semi-translucent material that has the effect of diffusing light.

**Open flash.** Technique of firing flash manually after the camera SHUTTER has been opened, instead of synchronizing the flash automatically.

**Optical axis.** Imaginary line through the optical centre of a lens system.

**Orthochromatic.** Term used to describe black-and-white EMULSIONS that are insensitive to red light. See also PANCHROMATIC.

**Oxidation.** Chemical reaction in which a substance combines with oxygen. Developer deteriorates through oxidation unless kept in airtight containers.

# P

**Pan-and-tilt head.** Type of tripod head employing independent locking mechanisms for movement in two planes at right angles to each other. Thus the camera can be locked in one plane while remaining free to move in the other.

**Panchromatic.** Term used to describe black-and-white photographic EMULSIONS that are sensitive to all the visible colours (although not necessarily equally to each of them). Nearly all modern films are panchromatic. See also ORTHOCHROMATIC.

**Panning.** Technique of moving the camera during EXPOSURE to follow a moving subject, giving an impression of speed. A relatively slow shutter speed is used, so that the background is more blurred than the subject.

**Panoramic camera.** Any camera that is capable of producing an image whose width is significantly wider than its height.

**Parallax.** The difference between what is seen through the viewfinder and what is recorded on the film. It occurs in non-SLR cameras where the viewfinder and the lens have slightly different viewpoints. It becomes a problem when shooting close-ups.

**Pentaprism.** Five-sided prism used in the construction of eye-level viewfinders for SLR cameras, which ensures that the image seen in the viewfinder is the right way round and the right way up. In practice the pentaprism often has more than five sides, as unnecessary parts of the prism are cut off to reduce its bulk.

**Permanence.** Permanence is determined initially by the effectiveness of the processing, and in colour photographs by the stability of the dyes in the emulsion layers. Development and fixing must be followed by thorough washing to remove all traces of those residual silver compounds that could affect the image's appearance. If prints are to be mounted, dry mounting is the most permanent method because it does not introduce any potentially harmful chemicals to the back of the print, as do many glues. When processed and stored carefully, black-and-white photographic materials will generally stay in good condition indefinitely. Colour images are less permanent, and are especially susceptible to direct sunlight. For maximum life expectancy, colour images should be stored in refrigerated conditions or as separation negatives.

**Phenidone.** Developing agent, usually used to stimulate the action of the chemical hydroquinone, in place of METOL. A small amount is very effective.

**pH value.** A scale used to measure the acidity or alkalinity of a substance. Pure water is neutral at pH 7; a smaller pH value than this indicates an acid, while a higher number indicates an alkali.

**Photoelectric cell.** Light-sensitive cell used in the circuit of a light meter. Some types of photoelectric cell generate an electric current when stimulated by light, others react by a change in their electrical resistance.

**Photoflood.** Bright tungsten filament bulb used as an artificial light source in photography. The bulb is over-run (to increase the brightness, more current passes through the filament than would in a standard bulb running for a longer period) and it therefore has a short life.

**Photogram.** Photographic image produced by arranging objects on the surface of a sheet of photographic paper or film, or so that they cast a shadow directly onto the material as it is being exposed. The image is thus produced without the use of a lens.

**Photometer.** Instrument for measuring the intensity of light by comparing it with a standard source.

**Photomicrography.** Technique of taking photographs through the lens of a microscope.

**Physiogram.** Photographic image of the pattern traced out by a light source suspended from a pendulum. The pattern depends on the arrangement and complexity of the pendulum.

**Pinhole camera.** Simple camera that employs a very small hole instead of a lens to form an image.

**Polarized light.** Light whose electrical vibrations are confined to a single plane. In everyday conditions, light is usually unpolarized, having electrical (and magnetic) vibrations in every plane. Light reflected from shiny non-metallic surfaces is usually polarized and can be controlled using a POLARIZING FILTER.

**Polarizing filters.** Thin transparent filters used as a lens accessory to cut down reflections for certain shiny surfaces (such as glass and water), or to intensify the colour of a blue sky (by reducing the amount of light reflected by the sky). Rotating the filter will vary the proportion of the polarized light that is blocked. There are two types of polarizing filter – linear and circular. Circular polarizing filters are constructed in a different way from linear polarizers so that they do not interfere with the exposure and autofocus systems of some cameras, and are therefore necessary when using autofocus SLRs.

**Positive.** Image in which the light tones correspond to the light areas of the subject, and the dark tones to the dark areas. In colour photography, it refers to an image in which the colours correspond to those of the original subject. See NEGATIVE.

**Positive lens.** See CONVERGING LENS.

**Posterization.** Technique of drastically simplifying the tones of an image by making several negatives from an original each with different densities and contrasts, and then sandwiching them together and printing them in register. The effect can also be achieved electronically.

**Primary colours.** Red, green and blue light. These can be mixed together to give white light, or in different proportions to each other to give light of any other colour.

**Process film.** A slow, fine-grained film of good resolving power that is used for copying work.

**Process lens.** Highly corrected lens designed specially for copying work.

**Pushing.** Technique that increases the effective SPEED of a film by extending its normal development time.

# R

**Rangefinder.** Optical device for measuring distance, sometimes coupled to the focusing system of a camera lens. A rangefinder displays two images, showing the scene from slightly different viewpoints, that must be superimposed one on the other to establish the subject's distance.

**Real image.** In optics, the term used to describe an image that can be formed on a screen, as distinct from a VIRTUAL IMAGE. The rays of light actually pass through the image before entering the eye of the observer.

**Reciprocity law.** Principle according to which the DENSITY of the image formed when the EMULSION is developed is directly proportional to the duration of the EXPOSURE and the intensity of the light. However, with extremely short or long exposures, and with unusual light intensities, the law fails, leading to unpredictable results, hence the term reciprocity failure. See also INTERMITTENCY EFFECT.

**Reducer.** Chemical agent used to reduce the DENSITY of a developed image either uniformly over the whole surface (leaving the contrast unaltered) or in proportion to the existing density (thus decreasing contrast). The best known is FARMER'S REDUCER.

**Reduction.** Technique for thinning an overdense negative or print with the aid of a chemical solution such as FARMER'S REDUCER, which bleaches away the silver image. Reduction can brighten small areas of a print, or rescue a muddy or overexposed print immersed in the solution. But reduction affects lighter tones first, thereby increasing contrast. After reduction the print must be fixed again and washed.

**Reflector.** Sheets of white, gold or silver material employed to reflect light into shadow areas.

**Reflex camera.** Generic name for types of camera whose viewing systems use a mirror to reflect an image onto the viewfinder screen. See also TWIN-LENS REFLEX and SINGLE-LENS REFLEX.

**Refraction.** Bending of a ray of light travelling obliquely from one medium to another; the ray is refracted at the surface of the two media.

**Rehalogenization.** The process of converting deposits of black metallic silver back into silver halides. This process may be used to bleach prints in preparation for toning. See also TONER.

**Resin-coated (RC) paper.** Photographic printing paper coated with synthetic resin to prevent the paper base from absorbing liquids during processing. Resin-coated papers can be washed and dried more quickly than untreated papers.

**Resolving power.** Ability of an optical system to distinguish between objects that are very close together.

**Reticulation.** Fine, irregular pattern appearing on the surface of an EMULSION that has been subjected to a sudden and severe change in temperature.

**Retina.** Light-sensitive layer at the back of the eye.

**Reversal film.** Photographic film that gives a positive image when processed. A film intended for producing slides, rather than negatives.

**Reversing ring.** A camera accessory that enables the lens to be attached to the camera back to front. Used in close-up photography to achieve a high magnification ratio.

**Ring flash.** Type of electronic flash unit that fits around the lens to produce flat, shadowless lighting. It is particularly useful in close-up work.

**Rising front.** One of the principal camera movements. The lens is moved vertically in a plane parallel to the film. It is particularly important in the field of architectural photography, as it allows the photographer to include the top of the building without causing CONVERGING VERTICALS to appear.

# S

**Sabattier effect.** Partial reversal of the tones of a photographic image resulting from a secondary EXPOSURE to light during the development process. Sometimes also know as SOLARIZATION or, more correctly, pseudo-solarization. A special effect usually carried out at the printing stage.

**Safelight.** Darkroom lamp whose light is of a colour (usually red or orange) that will not affect certain photographic materials. Safelight can be used with black-and-white printing paper, and with ORTHOCHROMATIC film. Colour

materials must, however, be handled in total darkness.

**Sandwiching.** The projection or printing of two or more negatives or slides together to produce a composite image.

**Saturated colour.** Pure colour, free from any mixture with grey.

**Selenium cell.** One of the principal types of photoelectric cell used in light meters. A selenium cell produces a current when stimulated by light, proportional to the intensity of the light.

**Separation negative.** A negative that records one of the three primary colours of a subject, or, more usually, a transparency, as a silver image. For photomechanical printing a set of three separation negatives is produced, recording the red, green and blue components respectively, together with a negative recording the tones of the whole scene. These are used to produce four plates in cyan, magenta, yellow and black and white.

**Shading.** Alternative term for DODGING.

**Shutter.** Camera mechanism that controls the duration of the EXPOSURE. The two main types of shutter are the BETWEEN-THE-LENS SHUTTER and the FOCAL-PLANE SHUTTER.

**Single-lens reflex (SLR).** One of the most popular types of camera. Its name is derived from its viewfinder system, which enables the user to see an image that is produced by the same lens as the one used for taking the photograph. A hinged mirror reflects this image onto a viewing screen, where the picture may be composed and focused. When the SHUTTER is released the mirror flips out of the light path, so that the film can be exposed. See also TWIN-LENS REFLEX.

**Silver halide.** Chemical compound of silver with a HALOGEN (for example, silver iodide, silver bromide or silver chloride). Silver bromide is the principal light-sensitive constituent of modern photographic emulsion, though other silver halides are also used.

**Slave unit.** Photoelectric device used to trigger electronic flash units in studio work. The slave unit detects light from a primary flash-gun linked directly to the camera, and fires the secondary flash unit to which it is connected.

**SLR.** Abbreviation for SINGLE-LENS REFLEX.

**Snoot.** Conical lamp attachment used to control the beam of a studio light.

**Soft focus.** Slight diffusion of the image achieved by use of a special FILTER or similar means, which softens the definition of the image. The effect is usually used to give a romantic haze to a photograph.

**Solarization.** Strictly, the complete or partial reversal of the tones of an image as a result of extreme overexposure. Often used to refer to the SABATTIER EFFECT, which produces results similar in appearance.

**Spectrum.** The multi-coloured band obtained when light is split up into its component WAVELENGTHS, as when a prism is used to split white light into coloured rays, the term may also refer to the complete range of electromagnetic radiation, extending from the shortest to the longest wavelengths and including visible light.

**Speed.** The sensitivity of an EMULSION to light. See ISO.

**Spherical aberration.** Lens defect resulting in an image that is not sharp, caused by light rays passing through the outer edges of a lens being more strongly refracted than those passing through the central parts. Not all rays, therefore, are brought to exactly the same focus.

**Spot meter.** Special light meter that takes a reading from a very narrow

ANGLE OF VIEW. In some TTL METERS the reading may be taken from only a small central portion of the image in the viewfinder.

**Spotting.** Retouching a print or negative to remove blemishes.

**Stabilization.** Chemical process of making the unexposed silver halides stable in prints. Used instead of fixing and washing when speed is more important than permanence.

**Standard lens.** Lens of FOCAL LENGTH approximately equal to the diagonal of the negative format for which it is intended. In the case of 35mm cameras the standard lens is a 50mm, for the 6 x 6cm (2¼ x 2¼ in) format it is an 80mm lens.

**Stop.** Alternative name for an APERTURE setting, or F NUMBER.

**Stop bath.** Weak acidic solution used in processing as an intermediate bath between the DEVELOPER and the FIXER. The stop bath serves to halt the development completely, and at the same time to neutralize the alkaline developer, thereby preventing it lowering the acidity of the fixer when it is added.

**Stopping down.** Term used for reducing the APERTURE of a lens.

**Subbing.** Coating a non-porous surface with a 5 per cent gelatin solution so that it will accept a photographic emulsion.

**Subminiature camera.** Camera using 16mm film to take negatives measuring 12 x 17mm (½ x ¾ in).

**Subtractive colour printing.** Principal method of filtration used in making prints from colour negatives. The colour balance of the print is established by exposing the paper through a suitable combination of yellow, magenta or cyan filters, which selectively block the part of the light giving rise to an unwanted colour cast. See also ADDITIVE COLOUR PRINTING.

**Supplementary lens.** Simple POSITIVE LENS used as an accessory for close-ups. The supplementary lens fits over the normal lens, producing a slightly magnified image.

## T

**Telephoto.** Lens (or lens setting) with a long FOCAL LENGTH and a small ANGLE OF VIEW.

**Test strip.** Print showing the effects of several trial EXPOSURE times, made in the darkroom to assess the correct exposure time.

**TLR.** Abbreviation of TWIN-LENS REFLEX camera.

**Tone separation.** Printing technique similar to POSTERIZATION, used to strengthen the tonal range in a print by printing the highlights and the shadows separately.

**Toner.** Chemical used to alter the colour of a black-and-white print.

**Transparency.** A photograph viewed by transmitted, rather than reflected, light. When mounted in a rigid frame, the transparency is called a slide.

**T setting.** Abbreviation of time setting. A setting available on some cameras for giving very long EXPOSURES. When the SHUTTER release is pressed, the shutter remains open until the release is pressed a second time. See also B SETTING.

**TTL meter.** Through-the-lens meter. Built-in EXPOSURE meter that measures the intensity of light in the image produced by the main camera lens. Principally found in SINGLE-LENS REFLEX cameras.

**Twin-lens reflex (TLR) camera.** Type of camera whose viewing system employs a secondary lens of FOCAL LENGTH equal to that of the main 'taking' lens. A fixed mirror reflects the image from the viewing lens up onto a ground glass screen. Twin-lens reflex cameras suffer

from PARALLAX error, particularly when focused at close distances. See also SINGLE-LENS REFLEX camera.

## U

**Ultraviolet radiation.** Electromagnetic radiation of wavelengths shorter than those of violet light, the shortest visible wavelength. They affect most photographic emulsions to some extent. See also INFRARED RADIATION.

**Universal developer.** Developing solutions for black-and-white materials that are intended for use with both films and printing papers.

**Uprating.** See PUSHING.

**UV filter.** Filter positioned over the camera lens to absorb ultraviolet radiation, which is particularly prevalent on hazy days. A UV filter enables the photographer to penetrate the haze with the camera to a certain extent.

## V

**Variable contrast (VC) paper.** Photographic printing paper sensitized in such a way that it can give a range of different contrast grades. Each grade is activated by a different coloured filter in the enlarger. The best-known paper of this sort is Ilford's MULTIGRADE. Multigrade's special emulsion has a mixture of two types of silver halide, one sensitive to blue light, the other to green light. Exposing the blue-sensitive part produces a high-contrast image; exposing the green-sensitive part produces a low-contrast image. Yellow filters are used to absorb blue light and transmit green, magenta filters to absorb green and transmit blue. An enlarger with a colour-mixing head can be used with Multigrade paper, but greater control is possible with special Multigrade filters.

**View camera.** Large-format studio camera whose viewing system consists of a ground-glass screen at the back of the camera on which the picture is composed and focused before the film is inserted. The front and back of the camera are attached by a flexible bellows unit, which allows a full range of camera movements.

**Viewfinder.** Window or frame on a camera showing the scene that will appear in the picture.

**Vignette.** Picture printed so the image fades gradually into the border area.

**Virtual image.** In optics, an image that cannot be obtained on a screen; a virtual image is seen by an observer in a position through which rays of light appear to have passed, but in fact have not. See also REAL IMAGE.

## W

**Water softeners.** Chemicals that remove or render harmless the calcium or magnesium salts present in 'hard' tap water. These impurities react with developers and may cause some to be deposited on films.

**Wavelength.** The distance between successive points of equals 'phase' on a lightwave; the distance, for example, between successive crests or troughs.

**Wetting agent.** Chemical that lowers the surface tension of water, often used in the final rinse (particularly of film) to promote even drying.

**Wide-angle lens.** Lens of FOCAL LENGTH shorter than that of a standard lens. A wide-angle lens, or lens setting, has a short focal length and a wide ANGLE OF VIEW.

**Working solution.** Processing solution diluted to the strength at which it is intended to be used. Most chemicals are sold in concentrate form, to save space.

## X

**X-rays.** Electromagnetic radiation with WAVELENGTHS very much shorter than those of visible light.

## Z

**Zone focusing.** Technique of presetting the APERTURE and focusing of the camera so that the entire zone in which the subject is likely to appear is covered by the DEPTH OF FIELD. This technique is particularly useful in areas of photography such as photojournalism and sport in which there is not time to focus the camera more accurately at the moment of taking the photograph.

**Zone system.** System of relating EXPOSURE readings to tonal values in picture-taking, development and printing, popularized by the American landscape photographer Ansel Adams.

**Zoom lens.** Lens with a variable FOCAL LENGTH, where the FOCAL PLANE remains unchanged while the focal length is being altered.

# Index

Page numbers in **bold** type refer to main entries.